T0155652

Design Thinking

Design Thinking is a set of strategic and creative processes and principles used in the planning and creation of products and solutions to human-centered design problems.

With design and innovation being two key driving principles, this series focuses on, but not limited to, the following areas and topics:

- User Interface (UI) and User Experience (UX) Design

- Psychology of Design

- Human-Computer Interaction (HCI)

- Ergonomic Design

- Product Development and Management

- Virtual and Mixed Reality (VR/XR)

- User-Centered Built Environments and Smart Homes

- Accessibility, Sustainability and Environmental Design

- Learning Design

- Strategy and best practices

This series publishes books aimed at designers, developers, storytellers and problem-solvers in industry to help them understand current developments and best practices at the cutting edge of creativity, to invent new paradigms and solutions, and challenge Creatives to push boundaries to design bigger and better than before.

More information about this series at https://link.springer.com/bookseries/15933.

A Guide to UX Design and Development

Developer's Journey Through the UX Process

Tom Green
Joseph Labrecque

Apress®

A Guide to UX Design and Development: Developer's Journey Through the UX Process

Tom Green
Toronto, ONTARIO, Canada

Joseph Labrecque
Thornton, CO, USA

ISBN-13 (pbk): 978-1-4842-9575-5
https://doi.org/10.1007/978-1-4842-9576-2

ISBN-13 (electronic): 978-1-4842-9576-2

Managing Director, Apress Media LLC: Welmoed Spahr
Acquisitions Editor: Divya Modi
Development Editor: James Markham
Editorial Assistant: Divya Modi

Cover designed by eStudioCalamar

Cover image designed by Pixabay

Distributed to the book trade worldwide by Springer Science+Business Media New York, 1 New York Plaza, Suite 4600, New York, NY 10004-1562, USA. Phone 1-800-SPRINGER, fax (201) 348-4505, e-mail orders-ny@springer-sbm.com, or visit www.springeronline.com. Apress Media, LLC is a California LLC and the sole member (owner) is Springer Science + Business Media Finance Inc (SSBM Finance Inc). SSBM Finance Inc is a **Delaware** corporation.

For information on translations, please e-mail booktranslations@springernature.com; for reprint, paperback, or audio rights, please e-mail bookpermissions@springernature.com.

Apress titles may be purchased in bulk for academic, corporate, or promotional use. eBook versions and licenses are also available for most titles. For more information, reference our Print and eBook Bulk Sales web page at http://www.apress.com/bulk-sales.

Any source code or other supplementary material referenced by the author in this book is available to readers on GitHub. For more detailed information, please visit https://github.com/Apress/A-Guide-to-UX-Design-and-Development-by-Tom-Green-Joseph-Labrecque.

Printed on acid-free paper

To Louie Morais

Table of Contents

About the Authors

Tom Green is a retired Professor of Interactive Multimedia through the School of Media Studies and IT at the Humber College Institute of Technology and Advanced Learning in Toronto, Canada. He has created over a dozen UX-based courses for LinkedIn Learning. One course—UX Design for Non-Designers, released 2 years ago—has been completed by over 35,000 learners throughout the world. Tom has written numerous books on UX design software for, among others, Apress, Que, Pearson Education, friendsofED, and New Riders. Along with his work with LinkedIn Learning, Tom has developed video-based training courses for Infinite Skills, Envato, Video2Brain, and others. He was the graphics software expert with the former About.com and has written hundreds of articles and tutorials for a variety of magazines and websites over the past 20 years. He has spoken and lectured at more than 50 international conferences and over a dozen universities throughout China and the United States, including the University of Wisconsin, Central Academy of Fine Arts in Beijing, Wuhan Institute of Technology, and Shenzhen Polytechnic. In his spare time, you can catch him hiking a local trail or paddling across a lake in Northern Ontario.

Joseph Labrecque is a creative developer, designer, and educator with nearly two decades of experience creating expressive web, desktop, and mobile solutions. He joined the University of Colorado Boulder College of Media, Communication and Information as faculty with the Department of Advertising, Public Relations and Media Design in Autumn 2019. His teaching focuses on creative software, digital workflows, user interaction, and design principles and concepts. Before joining the faculty at CU Boulder, he was associated with the University of Denver as adjunct faculty and as a senior interactive software engineer, user interface developer, and digital media designer.

Joseph has authored a number of books and video course publications on design and development technologies, tools, and concepts through publishers that include LinkedIn Learning, Apress, Peachpit, Packt, and Adobe. He has spoken at large design and technology conferences such as Adobe MAX and for a variety of smaller creative communities. He is also the founder of Fractured Vision Media, LLC, a digital media production studio and distribution vehicle for a variety of creative works.

Joseph is an Adobe Education Leader, Adobe Community Expert, and member of Adobe Partners by Design. He holds a bachelor's degree in communication from Worcester State University and a master's degree in digital media studies from the University of Denver.

About the Technical Reviewer

Kevin Brandon is a knowledgeable graphic designer, experience designer, professor, and speaker. Driven by the love of good design and creative exploration, he takes pride in finding solutions to problems. As a digital design expert, his goals are to keep up with the latest technology, collaborate with others, and express joy and humor in the creative process.

Acknowledgments

This being the 10th or 11th book I have written for Apress and an imprint it acquired a few years ago—friendsofED—I usually open with: "Working with a co-author can be a tricky business. In fact, it is a lot like a marriage. Everything is wonderful when things are going well, but you never really discover the strength of the relationship until you really get into it." This is not the case with Joseph.

Over the course of the past couple of decades, we have worked together on a number of projects for Adobe and others. Over that time, we have developed a rather close and professional relationship. When I first approached Joseph about our taking on this book, he, as only Joseph can, said, "Well, sure.... No problem." I honestly don't know how other author teams work, but Joseph and I make the ideal time. We would talk about an upcoming chapter in a 5-minute Zoom call, and 4 or 5 days later, Joseph would send in the chapter. We have become so close as authors, the tech editor for this book asked me, "Did you write this chapter?" I didn't tell him it was Joseph's. That is truly the mark of a great co-author and writer.

The genesis for this book was a statement I had made—"UX is nothing more than common sense"—in a LinkedIn Learning course. Somehow a couple of "names" in the UX field got hold of it, and... then the fight started. It was at this point Louie Morais contacted me to tell me to ignore them because I had gotten it right. From that Louie and I would trade long notes about the UX field. His most important revelation to me was "UX is both a mission and a process." The discussion resulting from that bit of wisdom has culminated in the book before you.

ACKNOWLEDGMENTS

Finally, thank you, Divya Modi, for having faith in this book. There were a couple of occasions where I essentially threw in the towel before we started, and Divya refused to accept that. When you work with an editor who so strongly believes in the book, you do all you can to validate their faith in the title. Thank you, Divya.

—Tom Green

This is the second Apress book I've co-authored with Tom. When he began making inquiries as to whether I'd like to take on this work, I was honestly a bit reluctant, not because I'd be working with Tom, of course, but because I had just authored an all-new book a few months before and was wrapping up work on a third edition book as well... which I honestly thought was too much already. I was, perhaps, in somewhat of a book burnout, mentally.

After giving it some days of consideration... swinging backward and forward... there were two things that drove my positive response to join up again and contribute to this book. The first is that Tom is always a great co-author. Whether collaborating on large books like this or even smaller video projects or article series, I've never had any issues or drama working with him, whatsoever.

The second reason I was willing to collaborate was in consideration of the topic and approach. As a longtime "hybrid" designer/developer... I am very familiar with all phases of the process we cover across these chapters. A few years back, I switched professions from one that was focused upon software engineering and product development... to full-time faculty teaching advertising and design students at a major university. When accepting the offer for this position, the department chair asked whether I might be interested in taking on a course that involved user experience and user interface design, in light of my previous life. In the years since, this class has morphed into a highly enjoyable experience for myself and for the media design students who participate in the course. Since this class aligns so well with the content of this present work... how could I say no? Additionally, the approach of this book is not the sort of step-by-step design or development projects that I normally write for other books—but, rather, is more open and conversational.

Thank you, Tom, for inviting me to participate in the creation of this book and especially for your friendship over the years.

—Joseph Labrecque

Introduction

There are times when the old adage "You can learn anything on the Internet!" does not exactly ring true. If you search for "learning UX," "UX design," or anything with that magical contraction—*UX*—in the search term or the name, you will be confronted with a bewildering plethora of acronyms, contradicting workflows, nonsensical job titles, and so on. It has gotten to the point with UX that if asked, "What is UX?", our response is, "What do you want it to mean?"

In many respects, the term "UX" has become devalued. There seems to be an assumption that if one tosses UX into a job description or position, the door to instant riches opens. This is simply not true. The job boards are awash with individuals claiming, for example, they are "UX designers" when, in fact, they have no idea of what a UX designer really does.

UX is user experience with emphasis on the word "*experience.*"

The genesis of this book is the day one of the authors tried to succinctly define the term when he said, "UX is nothing more than common sense." It sparked off a firestorm of criticism and debate that raged for well over two weeks. It was during this debate that Louie Morais, to whom this book is dedicated, told the author he was quite correct in that claim because it perfectly described what he called "the UX Mission." His point was there was an inability to separate the UX Mission from the UX Process. The Mission, according to Louie, is simple: *provide users with a great experience.* The Process, according to Louie, answers the question arising from that statement: *"How do we do that?"*

This book deals with both aspects of UX and the area where they intersect, which is "collaboration." It also focuses on an individual commonly overlooked in the UX Process—you, the developer.

Development is the end of the road for the UX Process, but it does not mean the assets are neatly bundled up and tossed over to the development team with a cheery "Here you go." We regard developers as critical team members who are involved in this collaborative UX Process right from the start of the UX journey.

Book Structure and Flow

This is not a software book. There is no common project that runs throughout the book other than using the development of a hypothetical parking lot application as the book's anchor. Instead, each chapter walks you through where the developer can and should be involved.

This is also not a book presenting the secrets to UX development, clever coding solutions, or even "how-tos." It does not focus on any UX design or development tool, and we studiously avoided any claims such as "This is the way it has to be done." Instead, think of this book as a general field manual that walks you through the entire UX Process right from the point where the inevitable first question around the process is asked: *How do we do that?*

We start by explaining what is meant by the UX Mission and the UX Process. By understanding how they are both separate and linked together, you should gain an understanding of what drives a UX project. We also make it quite clear the intersection of the Mission and the Process is where collaboration comes to life and becomes the subtext for the rest of the book.

Chapter 2 explores the role of the developer during the research phase of a project. You learn why you need to be involved. The reason is you get an intimate look at the user targets. With that information, you can start considering the impact this research will have on the system. From there we move into how the scope and minimum viable product (MVP) of the project are determined and your rather important role in this process.

The following chapters dig deeply into the design phase of a project, which starts when the research phase of the UX Process is completed and locked in. Throughout these chapters you will discover the role of a UX designer has nothing to do with design, and we outline a number of the creative team members and what they do prior to development. As you go through these chapters, you will discover your role is integral to the process as you grasp the "intent" of the project and can start planning the development phase of the project.

The final four chapters focus on the final phase of any UX project, development. They focus on the development workflow, user testing, handoff to development, and release of the project. You may think user testing should appear earlier in the book, and it does, but once the project is developed, it must be subjected to user testing, which will result in changes or a complete rethink of the project. The takeaway from this chapter is the term "user testing" is not correct. It is composed of two parts: user testing and usability testing. We also explain that "handoff" is not simply letting development take over. In fact, there is a process—Design > Develop > Test—that is constantly undertaken as you develop the project. The final chapter may surprise you because release does not mean you can move on to another project. In fact, the entire UX Process starts all over again as user data is analyzed.

Finally, we do not claim "This is the way you outta do it." That is nothing more than arrogance. There is no common team makeup or workflow. Instead, our intent is to show that you are an integral part of the UX Mission and the UX Process. Being involved in the entire process actually makes your job easier. The final takeaway from this book is that you, the developer, have a role within the team that is just as important as anyone else on the team.

CHAPTER 1

The UX Project Progress

Fall in love with the user... not the technology.

This was something one of us would tell his students during their very first day of class. He would, facetiously, add that they should tattoo that phrase inside their left eyelid. There was a reason for this.

When living in a world of design and development, it is all too easy to fall into the trap of focusing on the tools being used to design the project or the code libraries, languages, techniques, and so on used by developers in bringing the project to life. This was especially true when businesses and corporations awakened to the fact people were using their smartphones and tablets to access their goods, products, and services via their websites or, in a few instances, via these things called apps.

This user behavior was just so new nobody had a real grasp on how to build these things. Designers would cook up a wonderful design, chop it up, throw it into a folder, and hand it over to the developer with a cheery "Over to you." The designer would move on to the next project, and the developer would have all these pieces of an app or website and be left to assemble the project in such a way that it met what the developer assumed to be the project's intent. Often, they missed the mark, and when the users complained or simply abandoned the app, the needle on the Compass of Blame (Figure 1-1) inevitably swung to point at the developer.

© Tom Green and Joseph Labrecque 2023
T. Green and J. Labrecque, *A Guide to UX Design and Development*, Design Thinking,
https://doi.org/10.1007/978-1-4842-9576-2_1

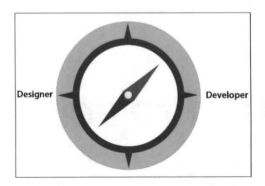

Figure 1-1. *The Compass of Blame*

There is no clear point in time where that all changed, but the year 2010 would be a good starting point. Apple had introduced the iPhone, Flash Player disappeared from the iOS universe, HTML5 was in development, and shortly thereafter... Apple introduced the App Store and Google released the Android operating system (OS). Over the following years as the budgets, along with the financial risk, seriously increased, a collaborative environment emerged, and teams expanded to include social scientists whose job was to determine if there was a need for a product, who would use it, and why. Other skills such as motion design, user interface (UI) design, and accessibility also started appearing on project teams.

At various points in the product design and development cycle, these scientists would sit down with people representing the intended consumer audience and evaluate whether the project was a "go" for market release. Once again, the developers would be in the unenviable position of having that Compass of Blame point in their direction if the results of user research were mulled over, and the responsibility to fix the UX was dropped in their laps. This has all changed simply because the tolerance for financial risk has decreased and the whole field of user experience (UX) has proven to be more than a buzzword but has grown to become, as one of the authors loves to say, "a team sport."

Though the focus of today's current UX environment is on design, developers are increasingly taking a seat at the table and are expected to actively participate in the product design process from concept to release into the wild. What this means is developers are just as important to the design process as everyone else because they build the ideas that come to fruition. What changed?

Developers were traditionally perceived as solitary coders specializing in one technology or another. Now developers are the designers of code across a stack of technologies. As such, like the protagonist hero in *The Pilgrim's Progress*, the developer now also co-owns the product design journey, from that initial meeting in a boardroom where the discovery research is presented to the team to the delivery of a solution and all eventual changes and fixes required once that solution is used by real human beings after it went live.

The UX Mission

The term "UX" is so commonly misused that when asked to define it, we'd turn it around and ask, "What do you want it to mean?" The term has become a jumble of contradictory definitions to the point where "UX" is being confused with the job practices of everyone ranging from graphic artists to front-end developers. So let's clear that up right now.

User experience is both a process and a mission (Figure 1-2), and they are distinctly different aspects from one another.

Figure 1-2. *UX has two interlocked aspects*

The UX Process is the workflow from initial research and conceptualization to upload, distribution, and user engagement in the wild. This aspect requires several specialized skills, which may include UX researchers, designers, writers, motion designers, interactivity designers, and developers. The process involves a lot of software tools, brainstorming, and planning with all of it moving in a straight line to an iterative product.

The UX Mission goes above all of that. It focuses on the person who will load the product onto their device or open it on a web page. It focuses on making life easier for that person in such a way that they will continue using the product. In short, the mission is, as we said right at the top of this chapter, to fall in love with the user.

Let's explore this with a hypothetical example.

A local government has hundreds of parking lots scattered across the city, and the Parking Authority has received thousands of complaints about meters (Figure 1-3) and kiosks that either don't work as expected, are difficult to understand, or are out of order. Some accept credit cards, others only accept cash, and so on. We've all been there. At this point, the

Parking Authority realizes they have a huge problem and decide to create an app in an attempt to untangle this Gordian knot and make life easier for people with similarly frustrating experiences.

Figure 1-3. *The Mission: put this in our customers' smartphones*

This is where the Mission becomes critical.

A UX research firm is retained to collate the feedback the local government has already received and survey or interview the people that use the parking system. With all of this research data in hand, it is time to determine whether a parking app would solve their local taxpayers' problems.

Key questions to be answered would be "What are the demographics of people that use the parking lots?", "Where would they use it?", "How often would they use it?", "How would users prefer to pay for parking?", "What device would they use?" In short, the research is going to reveal insights from the very people who will use the app instead of the team or the client making broad internal or personal assumptions and moving on. Those insights will drive the process, which focuses on solving problems for users... not adding to them.

To be successful, the team, regardless of size, needs to effectively communicate with each other right from the start. The process requires the workload to be distributed... but success ultimately results from everyone maintaining a close relationship with everyone on the team. Even though the designers may not fully understand the development cycle—and vice versa—they must treat each other as members of the same production team. If that doesn't take hold, the project will fall victim to unnecessary compromises (scope creep, feature bloat), which will result in some very nasty feedback from users if not even outright failure of the project as users abandon the app and look for a competing app.

Why UX Projects Fail

To examine why projects fail, we can't simply point the Compass of Blame's needle toward either designers or developers. It is simply a case of regarding design and development as two solitudes. Although perceptions have changed, it is useful to look at how these two solitudes used to think and operate before they got brought into the UX way of doing things.

We'll start with you, the developer. When handed the assets, your focus used to be: "How do I make this thing work?" This resulted in viewing the project from the perspective of the system and looking for clever coding solutions to the task at hand. There was also a focus on scalability around how the system would increase or decrease in performance as it responded to system and processing demands. For example, in the case of the parking app, the focus would be on accommodating a rapid increase in users as the application got used or people set up accounts. In both cases, the priority was set on the technical aspects instead of the needs of the people who would use the app or the objectives of the business.

Designers didn't get off all that easy either. Finding themselves thrust into an Agile UX Process was like being dropped onto a deserted island. It was completely foreign to them as they quickly discovered Agile development never accounted for UX design. It was more geared toward software development, which resulted in the inevitable tension between the designers and the developers. This was brought home to one of the authors when he sat in on a presentation at a user group meeting. The presenter bubbled about all of the slick code that was written for the project and then, as an afterthought, said, "Then we brought in the designers to add the graphics and text."

To this point, the designer's focus was on making everything look great. Their focus was on aesthetics, and the code and technology were over there, on the other side, and it was the developer's job to make it work. In short, the designer was unconcerned with the developer's effort, and the developer wasn't concerned with the designer's effort. As long as it looked great and it worked, the project was a success.

Enter the UX Mission

When designers and developers worked apart from each other, it should come as no surprise both concentrated on the task at hand with little or no regard for the person who would download the app or visit the website and use it.

The walls crumbled not because reason between the two solitudes broke out but because the people using the app or website loudly complained or voted with their browsers or devices and simply went elsewhere.

We have all had the experience of trying to pay for something and having to hunt down how to do that or being asked to provide information that had nothing to do with paying for something. We've all had the experience of having to wait for an inordinate amount of time for a process to complete. Those horror stories, and more, are all too common as are abandoned shopping carts, cancelled accounts, and being called out on social media. They all have a financial cost and contribute to the reasons most startups fail. There is a lot of good money funding bad ideas because the ideas don't focus on the user. They have ignored the UX Mission.

The user experience process embraces a mission that starts with understanding the point that will determine whether your efforts and time will be fruitful and add to your professional portfolio or are wasted because the product or service did not meet the needs of potential users.

As we progress in our journey, we will learn more about the importance of starting with user research to provide the insights that will guide developers, designers, and stakeholders in the creation of a parking app that might solve the issues raised by the local Parking Authority's users. You might not have realized it... but you already started taking on the UX Mission when, without thinking about any code, you just read about the hypothetical issues people have been encountering with the current parking meters.

The Collaborative UX Process

A keyword that you are going to encounter in the subsequent chapters is "collaboration." If done collaboratively, the process will be as smooth as silk. If done in silos, there is space for serious unforeseen consequences.

There is a cautionary tale about this in an article Paul Boag wrote for *Smashing* around a suggested change to Digg.com (Figure 1-4).

The lead designer came up with a rather interesting idea to change the site's Digg button. From a design point of view, this was a "no-brainer"— make the change and life is grand. That was until the lead developer dug into the suggestion and quickly realized this "no-brainer" change would require a major reformat of the code architecture and server setup. Needless to say, that "no-brainer" was killed when the lead developer explained all of this to the lead designer.

Paul Boag / NOV 21, 2014 / 81 comments

Why You Should Include Your Developer In The Design Process

📅 6 min read   🏷 Business, Workflow, Teams   🐦 Share on Twitter, LinkedIn

QUICK SUMMARY ↝ *Should designers be able to code? This topic never seems to die, with its endless blog posts, Twitter discussions and conference talks. But the developer's involvement in the design process seems to be addressed very little. This is a shame, because developers have a huge amount to add to discussions about design.*

Should designers be able to code? This topic never seems to die, with its endless blog posts, Twitter discussions and conference talks. But the developer's

ABOUT THE AUTHOR

Paul is a leader in conversion rate optimisation and user experience design thinking. He has over 25 years experience working with clients

Figure 1-4. Digg almost had a bad experience (www.smashingmagazine.com/2014/11/why-you-should-include-your-developer-in-the-design-process/)

Collaboration is the DNA of the UX Process, but there is a difference between collaboration and "design by committee." Without a flow of communication to negotiate the compromises between design aesthetics and technical requirements, there is a very real risk of diluting the design to satisfy everyone involved.

There is another benefit to collaboration. As you work more closely with the design members of the team, a degree of personal chemistry will inevitably take hold. The relationships you develop with designers and researchers will pay off in terms of having access to testing your hypothesis and knowing first-hand when your ideas hold true or not with the real users in user testing before you spend the time assembling them.

Finally, get ready to compromise and don't take anything personally. Nowadays, you don't have to passionately defend an idea in matters that are open for experimentation. The point is that until backed by user insight and data, we are all working with hypotheses of what could work—and developers are welcome to volunteer their hypotheses too.

You need to understand that team collaboration doesn't magically happen. It is a messy process and requires a lot of initiative and engagement from everyone involved so that product design moves from isolated practices done by siloed teams with competing agendas to a process where everyone involved clearly understands they are working on the same project regardless of role and that each phase of the project is just important as the next one. The view now becomes long-range. Instead of focusing on short-term objectives such as deliverables, the ultimate objective becomes the final product that will be put into people's hands. With an understanding of the team's composition and how it must collaborate, let's take a step back and take a broad look at the UX Process.

A Brief Review of the UX Process

Though there are countless articles and so on that explain the process, it can be broken down into five phases. They are the following.

Discovery and Problem Definition

The process starts with the discovery of how things work now and the negative and positive impacts of the current system on users and the business. Insight can be collected from analytics, feedback, and previous research. In many cases, more research is usually required to understand the specific areas that are candidates to change. In many cases, the data not only confirms the area chosen by the business requirements but also highlights other issues and needs that were not so obvious. These insights, deeper problems, and a clearer picture of who the users are and what they need are invaluable.

This phase is also called the problem(s) definition phase, and normally, these are the artifacts and deliverables used and produced and could include a full presentation of the research results, use case scenarios, and personas as shown in Figure 1-5.

Laura Guillfoyle

ABOUT

Laura is a freelance software engineer that lives in Sault Ste. Marie, Ontario. She prefers to be active in her free time and weekends are spent hiking or camping. Laura is an active sports enthusiast and prefers to attend Cross Fit and yoga classes at least once a week.

DEMOGRAPHICS:

AGE: 28
JOB: Self Employed
INCOME: $80k
EDUCATION: Software Engineer
LOCATION: Sault Ste. Marie, Ontario

GOALS

• Discovering new places.
• Attaining a high level of fitness
• Learning new things

FRUSTRATIONS:

• Poor trail maps.
• Poorly maintained campsites.
• Forgetting about recommendations

HABITS:

• Never leaves without a topographic map.
• Compulsive ebook reader.
• Constantly scanning Amazon to find new gear.
• Constantly updating her hiking blog.

MOTIVATIONS:

Incentive   ● ● ● ● ●
Achievement ● ● ● ● ●
Growth   ● ● ● ● ●
Social   ● ● ● ● ●

"I have always been passionate about exploring the wilderness of Northern Ontario. The lakes, rivers and forests surrounding Lake Superior are where I go to indulge my passion."

Figure 1-5. *Personas are deliverables (persona template from Figma using the PhotoSplash plugin)*

Scope and MVP Definition

Ideally, the minimum viable product (MVP) definition, usually locked and decided before it reaches the design phase, should be fluid and ongoing so that the insights from research and data found in the discovery phase define the final MVP or, at least, are earmarked for the very next iterations.

A series of prioritization sessions should follow up after discovery to align business, development, and design. Already at kickoff, development and design should be talking to each other, understanding each other's constraints and priorities, and negotiating those in favor of users and the business against risks, dependencies, and feasibility.

Normally, these are the artifacts and deliverables used and produced during this phase and could include wireframes (Figure 1-6), low-fidelity (LoFi) prototypes, and user journeys.

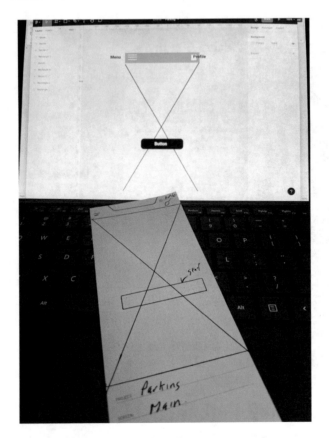

Figure 1-6. The project scope takes shape as wireframes are drawn on paper or software

UX Design

When the UX design phase starts, what usually happens is developers and designers disappear into their caves and weeks later emerge again for the wireframe and visuals handover. By then, it is too late. Designers and developers should be working together to evaluate the ideas and hypotheses both groups have presented, agreeing the designs are technically feasible because technical feasibility allows for an effective design for the user.

As you will see in the following chapters, the opportunities (and the need) for collaboration and weekly communication between designers, developers, and business just increase in the UX design phase: with the review of wireframed journeys, the evolution of a prototype to test the team's hypotheses, and the preparation for the user testing (Figure 1-7) that would review whether the designs solve the user issues found during the discovery phase. Normally, these are the artifacts and deliverables used and produced during this phase.

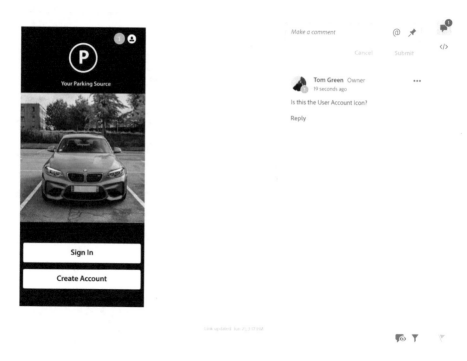

Figure 1-7. *Prototyping applications allow the team to view and comment to identify issues*

UI Design

As you know, as a developer you will be busy preparing the whole infrastructure that will hold the new system, but when you embrace the UX Mission, after testing the prototype, you will have not only a confirmation of what you are going to develop but the realization of how much time you and your team have saved by not launching yourselves into coding immediately after the scope was defined. Had you started coding then, you would have risked coding for a solution that would not have addressed what you now know (Figure 1-8).

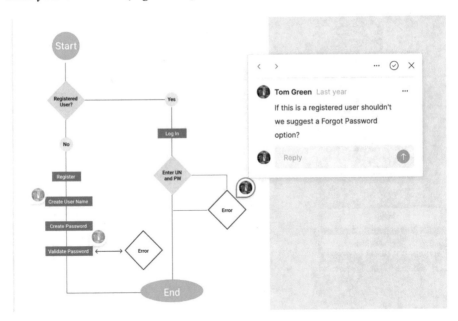

Figure 1-8. *Identifying issues before they become real issues*

As you get started prepping the back-end structure and logic, your voice as a full-stack developer or that of your specialized front-end developers in your team is still useful to guide the UI designers to produce designs that are scalable and utilize previously created designs that by now are part of your design system.

You will want to follow the UI design just as closely, as at the last minute you might realize that the UI designer completely forgot (or wasn't told) to cover the edge case scenarios that you end up having to solve alone, just to have them reverted at the last minute because your design decisions didn't match the best practices and patterns the UX team has been following according to known industry best practices and previous user insights.

Development

Once the development team has received all the front-end design deliverables, you might eventually discover dependencies and blockers that were not apparent when you first reviewed the wireframes and designs. In the past, developers too often decided to adapt the designs themselves fearing that once the UX and UI designers had thrown their deliverables over the fence to the development team and disappeared, the window to get designers to rethink their designs was closed.

As a result, developers invested time and effort to do things themselves just to have them corrected again by the design team in the next sprint, having their initiative misinterpreted as an act of excluding the design team. The point is that every time developers and designers miss an opportunity to collaborate and communicate as one team with a common goal to deliver a solution for users and business, both sides have to redo their work and waste time over things that could be agreed upon to and quickly fixed.

Deep Dive into the UX Process

With a high-level overview out of the way, let's look at those five phases in action.

Discovery and definition start with a few brainstorming sessions focused on how this app will look and function. All of this is based on the research data and the concepts and ideas presented by everyone—designers, developers, and researchers. As sessions progress, these concepts and ideas will get honed down from the wild to the specific. The key here is to identify and resolve issues related to both design and development giving everyone a chance to point out issues from their side of the fence.

For example, users may be required to enter their vehicle's license plate number. As the developer, it is reasonable to ask if it is just the number or if they should include state, province, or region as well. Another great developer issue would be asking how the parking inspectors access that particular vehicle's parking status because it may require pairing the app's session data with a device the attendant may be using to scan a license plate. These are not the issues one would want to encounter after the app is released. With that out of the way, the team can move on to the scope and MVP definition phase. This is not where you break out computers or notebooks and start drawing or prototyping. The whole purpose here is to prioritize features and ideas. Think of it as a laundry list of ideas to be organized individually based on feasibility and purpose. That list is then rearranged based on priority. This is where you need to be cold-blooded. For example, the initial consensus might be that an onboarding sequence would be a good idea. At this point, a member of the research team points out that the research indicates users are in a hurry and simply want to park their car and get on with their day. Suddenly, a really neat feature drops to the bottom of the list.

There are any number of ways of developing the priorities, and your organization will use a method best suited to your organization. A very simple method is to plot each idea on a priority/feasibility matrix (Figure 1-9).

Each idea is rated by each member of the team using a score of 1–5 based on priority and feasibility. The scores are then plotted with feasibility on the X-axis and priority on the Y-axis. As a developer, you now have a clear idea of the features to be included, but also you have been involved in that process and understand why they were included. We also might add this will be the start of the documentation process.

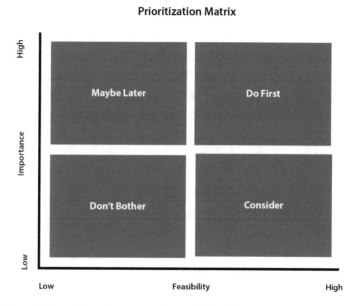

Figure 1-9. *Prioritization matrix used by UXPin*

With the features set, the time has arrived to assemble a realistic plan. This is where the work gets underway. A great place to start is with a review of the top-priority items. At this point, the entire team will need to review both the technical and functional specifications and document them. Just keep in mind this document is a starting point, not some sort of checklist. As a developer, you are the ultimate reality check. A must-have feature may have the total support of the team, but if you discover that feature is impossible to build, now is the time to kill it.

The project plan is commonly broken into phases along with what needs to be done. Think of this as a plan of attack outlining what needs to be done, by when, and by whom. Again, this plan becomes an integral part of the project documentation set. In no particular order, these phases could include

- *Wireframes*: These are low-fidelity ideas (LoFi)—boxes and arrows that allow the team to start building a structure and exploring UX concepts. These are easily done on paper or using software because if it doesn't work or get team "buy-in," they can get tossed into the nearest wastepaper basket or moved to the Trash. Once completed, it is not unheard of to create paper prototypes of the wireframes and send them out for user testing.

  Let's assume the team has agreed there will be a main screen where users log in to access the home screen where they can get to work. The initial wireframe may look like the crude representation shown in Figure 1-10. The plan is to have a welcome screen where the user taps a button to go to the login screen, and from there it is off to the home screen.

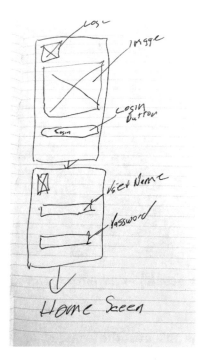

Figure 1-10. *A simple wireframe*

As the developer, your wireframe might look like
Figure 1-11. Essentially you are crudely mapping out
the logic and processes that get the user to the home
screen. This could be done on a wall, a whiteboard,
or even a notebook that is photographed and sent to
the team. It could also be done with the team.

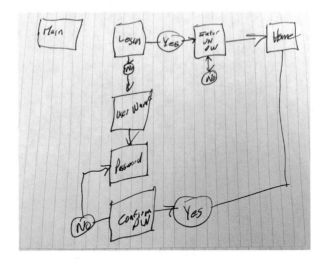

Figure 1-11. *A quick developer wireframe supporting the team's*
wireframe

What is going on here is the team saying, "We see it
happening this way" and you saying, "Here's how I
can make it happen."

At this point, you can move into the UX design phase
of the process where iteration and collaboration
become extremely important.

YOUR TURN

Open your smartphone and open an app. Break out a sheet of paper or
notebook and, using nothing more than squares, rectangles, arrows and
circles, sketch how you would redesign the home screen and the next screen
you would normally go to. Now sketch out a wireframe showing how you
would more efficiently enable the user to get from that first screen to the
second screen.

- *Prototyping*: In many respects, these can be regarded as medium-fidelity (MidFi) documents, and they commonly come in two flavors: static and interactive. Static prototypes can be created in such design applications as Sketch or Photoshop and contain the screens and assets used throughout the projects. The MidFi prototype essentially moves all of the static assets into a prototyping application such as Adobe XD, UXPin, or Figma where interactivity simply moves between the screens. There is also the high-fidelity (HiFi) prototype where interactivity, transitions, motion, effects, and so on are added.

The MidFi prototype (Figure 1-12) should be circulated to the entire team, including stakeholders, for feedback and should not be regarded as the final product's design. They are the designer essentially asking, "This is how we see the screens. What do you think?" As a developer, this is not only your opportunity to get an understanding of the assets that are going to be handed to you but also a chance to start thinking about how you will build the pages and how they will affect the system's operation. It is also, quite common, for the static prototypes to be sent out for user testing and for major and minor changes to be made based on user feedback. The interactive prototype allows everyone to "kick the project's tires." From a developer's point of view, the prototyping application will also allow you to introspect the underlying code supplied by the application, which, as the developer, you can choose to use or not use. Again, it is quite common to send this prototype out for user testing and for major or minor changes to be made to the project based on user feedback from both the users and the team.

Figure 1-12. *A medium-fidelity prototype prepared in Sketch*

- *Front-end development*: This is the work that precedes prototyping. The design assets are created, a design system is put in place, procedures for managing data are developed, browser support is addressed, and even animations and the JSON, CSS, or JavaScript code driving them are either created or shared with the development team.

- *User testing*: This is not a "one and done" thing done at the end. It is a continuous process involving not only users but the team at every step of the process. This is where the term "messy" really takes hold. Every test will

require major and minor changes. This is why there will
be several iterations of the project based on user and
team feedback. That's the bad news. The good news?
The number of iterations will decrease as the project
comes closer to completion, but there will always be
changes.

The prototypes have been created and shared, and they have been user
tested and changes made based on user feedback. The entire team has
also been involved to ensure the prototype remains faithful to the issues
discovered during the research phase. As well, the prototype retains its
fidelity to the plan and the feature set agreed to by the stakeholders. It is
time for the developer to become actively involved in the UI design phase.

Your involvement happens on two fronts: assets and the front-end
structure and logic. The assets will include all of what we call "the bits
and pieces of the prototype." This will include access to the design system,
design patterns, images, components, and other media found in the HiFi
prototype. Just keep in mind this HiFi prototype both is disposable and is
to be used as a guide to intent. This guide to intent is commonly provided
by the prototyping applications that include a developer view when the
prototype is shared with the team (Figure 1-13).

Figure 1-13. *Prototyping applications usually include a developer view such as this from Adobe XD*

Just be aware that Agile UX methodologies mean the designers work ahead of the developers. This is where your input into every step of the process is critical. Development is essential here to help inform the team about platform incompatibilities and limitations, API calls, and other things that might hinder or slow down a page or screen. Design needs to be ahead of development to make sure iterations can happen if needed. This is often referred to as DesignOps and DevOps, but there is one fundamental difference. The perceived walls between designers and developers are torn down. Instead, they are joined together with an unbreakable link, which is the user.

Conclusion

In this chapter, you have discovered that UX is composed of two parts: the Mission and the Process. The Mission is laser-focused on making the project easy to use, regardless of operating system, device, and data management structures. The Process is how the project comes to life and how each member of the team works in a collaborative environment where communication between teams is critical. You also learned the process is "messy" in that it involves multiple iterations of the project based on both user and team feedback, and this includes the stakeholders.

The chapter finished with a rough sketch of the process ranging from wireframe sketches to interactive prototypes that are put in front of the users and the team to ensure the UX Mission is being achieved and to identify issues that are impeding the mission and resolve them.

Finally, you have glimpsed the developer's progress, in a very broad context, through the UX Mission and the UX Process. As you have seen, your participation, suggestions, and input are just as invaluable as those whose roles are not development-oriented. It is incumbent upon you, as the developer, to point out such things as API calls that might affect a screen or web page.

As we pointed out right at the start of the chapter, UX is a team sport. Designers need an awareness of how the interfaces work, and this awareness will ripple through the entire UX Process. Similarly, you, the developer, have to become familiar with the design language, design systems, and style guides that visually communicate their intent. To achieve this, open collaboration and clear communication are the best way to move through the UX Process because everyone is focused on the UX Mission.

From this point on, this book will provide you with a deeper understanding of your role in both the UX Mission and UX Process. This all starts with your role right at the start of the UX Process where the concept is finalized and you identify the processes and so on that support the concept. We'll see you there.

CHAPTER 2

Defining the Problem

A well-defined problem will successfully inform and direct everything necessary to solve it.

Defining the problem your project is attempting to solve *correctly* is perhaps the most influential aspect of the entire process. If you define the problem incorrectly... you, as the developer, will have difficulty working around the issues these incorrect definitions have introduced—but your entire team will also suffer from this misstep. Of course—and thankfully—defining the problem is not a developer's responsibility alone. Everyone who is invested in the project needs to contribute to such an important task, and the results are most successful when this is achieved together—as a team effort.

In this chapter, we will explore many considerations around researching and defining the problems that must be addressed in this process. We'll emphasize why the research process is so crucial for developers to be a part of and why research should never end once you've come to a set of initial conclusions. We'll also examine how findings from successful research can influence the choice of platforms and systems, how this is intimately tied to what occurs on the front end, and why this affects the designers working on the project. Furthermore, we'll examine what considerations can even be taken in these early steps when considering assets and deliverables to further enhance and guide the UX

© Tom Green and Joseph Labrecque 2023
T. Green and J. Labrecque, *A Guide to UX Design and Development*, Design Thinking,
https://doi.org/10.1007/978-1-4842-9576-2_2

Process. Finally, we'll wrap up with some thoughts about the developer's role in the research process and why it is so beneficial to everyone to have a developer's involvement early on in the process.

We firmly believe a well-defined problem will successfully inform and direct everything necessary to solve it.

Why Research Is Important for Developers

Consider just about any other situation in life... Some examples might include teaching a class or workshop, giving a presentation at a major speaking event, or even organizing a get-together for an old friend. In any of these situations, you will take time to consider your audience, specific goals, the different options and approaches available to you, and what additional factors surrounding the circumstances might impact your approach and the response of others to that approach. Proper research is no different, and just as in the example scenarios... you'll be much more prepared and achieve a greater level of confidence in what you are doing if you take the necessary time to research and prepare before taking any additional actions.

Most prominently, this research will provide the information necessary to establish a clear trajectory for the project in a balanced and holistic way. Perhaps it is found that a competing product has a specific focus, leaving other functionality areas in a weaker position. The research demonstrates from user reviews that most users mention this weakness in the competitor experience. This could be the perfect opportunity to consider how your team might take advantage of this by strengthening a similar aspect in your own product—perhaps even luring users from the competing application.

Take our parking kiosk, for example. Perhaps it is discovered that a product exists that enables users to park their cars using the same system through an existing app on their mobile devices. It would benefit your team to install and use the app in the research phase to determine any immediate strengths and weaknesses first-hand. Your team can also research user reviews on mobile app stores to discover what users like and do not like about the existing app experience.

Gathering this data, the team can then identify what might be a good focus for your product vs. the competitor's experience (Figure 2-1). If weaknesses can be detected at this phase of the process, it can help direct a clear channel of what to continue to focus upon moving forward and also reveal, perhaps, areas where the team doesn't need to waste much time.

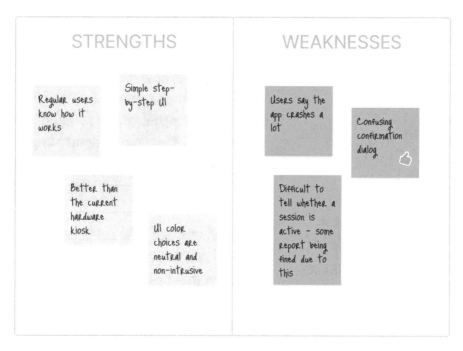

Figure 2-1. *Plotting strengths and weaknesses in a competing product*

Additionally, research will benefit the developer by providing greater insight into other stakeholders who are part of the overall process. This group consists of the users you are building the product for, the designers you are working with, and other groups who invest in the process, such as the project management team and company leadership.

Research done well will expose any weaknesses in the workflows under consideration and any designer or developer bias that currently exists and allow the development team to pivot early and adjust these workflows in cooperation with other teams to suit the users' needs better. In terms of the design and development process, these exposed weaknesses are best tackled by eliminating or reducing any silos within the business to establish a healthy dialogue among all stakeholders.

Early communication with the researchers and the design team will inform the development process and benefit everyone involved with a much richer communication system. Furthermore, this richness in collaboration and sharing will likely extend far beyond the initial research phase and will exist throughout the entire UX Process from beginning to end. This can be massively helpful to designers and developers since the research will remain fluid and continuous throughout the process, and if the teams remain confined within their silos... there can be devastating miscommunications in the direction and choices being made further along in the process.

Tip   An exercise that one of your authors often asks students in his UX and UI class is to perform a critical analysis exercise. The students will consider an app they are familiar with—that they use regularly—and write a short analysis, which identifies the experience's strengths and weaknesses. This could be a website, a mobile app, or even the interface for an automobile dashboard, exercise bike, or refrigerator. They are encouraged to use specific examples with screen captures or photographs to illustrate and back up each point that is put forth. An exercise such as this can help developers understand what to consider when researching specific experiences and can assist with inter-team dialogue within any organization.

Foundational Research Is Necessary

We've established why research is vital for developers to be involved in, but there are generally two phases of research to consider in any project... and both are necessary. The first phase of research will typically occur before anything else can happen as part of the process, before any design work, development, infrastructure decisions, or even choices around what features to include in the product. This first set of information-gathering is known as foundational research. The purpose of this research is just that— to establish a solid foundation that other phases of the overall UX Process can be reliably built upon (Figure 2-2).

Figure 2-2. *Foundational research will include a varied number of proven sources*

The idea behind foundational research activities is to establish a reliable data set to inform the process moving forward. Everyone involved likely has assumptions, personal bias, ideas, and expectations for the product, and many of them are probably misinformed or just plain wrong. This is because everyone has their own experiences and opinions.

Research, done well, can assist significantly in shifting perspectives and getting everyone to start thinking about the project from the same place. If you do not participate in foundational research as a developer, you are missing out on this major opportunity to guide the entire process from beginning to end.

The primary methods of foundational research are as follows:

- *Existing data*: This can include the gathering of data through analytics, surveying the competitions' products, looking over user reviews, noting and logging complaints that are posted on social networks, and assembling all of this data in one place. In our parking kiosk example, this could take the form of any published analytics from the kiosk company or researching reviews from existing digital methods of processing reservation and payment.

- *User interviews*: Since the user—or potential user—is really the focus of this entire process, it makes good sense to include them in any foundational research that is performed. Bringing in a potential user or even users of the competition's product and having a discussion with them is a great way to gather first-hand data that can inform your entire process.

- *Hands-on fieldwork*: This type of research involves you going out into the field and personally conducting exploratory research. With digital properties, this will often involve you installing an app or visiting a website to experience what others have experienced before you. In our parking kiosk example, it would involve parking your vehicle at a variety of parking lots and using the kiosk to experience it for yourself.

Of course, there may be additional sources to draw from depending upon the project itself, but these three are generally the most common and provide a reliable set of findings when considered together as a full data set, once the foundational research phase concludes. Once this foundational work is completed, stakeholders can assemble and pour over the data that has been gathered to better make decisions of what steps to take next and which features to include in a potential product. It is important to note, though, that even with this initial research phase concluded, there are great benefits to continuing your research throughout each of the phases within the entire process.

Tip   When considering the outcomes of foundational research inquiries and investigations, it can be easy to put more weight on certain sources of information while considering others to be inferior. Decision-makers should try and give each source of data equal footing when making decisions following the evaluation of this initial research. You never know what unexpected conclusions you may discover—and weighing certain sources over others can influence and corrupt the findings.

The Research Process Is Continuous

While thorough research is nearly always the first step in determining the problem and how to best approach it, that doesn't mean this aspect of the process can be safely tossed aside once you think you've gathered enough data. Things often change during the design and development process, which can help inform and contribute to existing and new areas of research for your project. These new developments can hold dramatic influence over the direction and approach of the design and development teams. To ignore or discount additional research at any phase of the process is likely to be a point of regret later down the line.

Of course, the bulk of the research should be done before many other aspects of the UX Process—as the findings from this initial research phase will determine what direction other steps take and where your team should focus the most resources. However, the research should continue in parallel to other steps in the UX Process and should even carry through past the product launch.

As the design and development work continues, targeted research (Figure 2-3) can provide insights that may not be apparent at the very beginning of the process, and post-launch research is critical to understanding how the users are responding to the product in day-to-day use. Real user data is most valuable in determining the success or failure of the decisions made throughout the project lifecycle and can not only help improve future versions of the product... but can help your team refine the process in future projects as well... improving overall success and confidence within your organization.

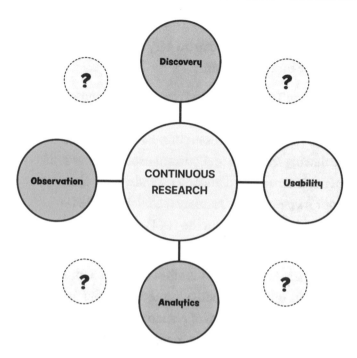

Figure 2-3. *Various research method types should be used continually across the entire UX Process, and all stakeholders should remain open to new types as dictated by the research results*

As for which research method types your team chooses to focus on during this continuous process, four often-employed categories are discovery, usability, analytics, and observation. These tie in very closely and even overlap with the foundational research types we looked at earlier. Let's examine each of these method types and where they might fit into the research process when considering our parking kiosk:

- *Discovery*: This type of research is normally the first task that is undertaken, as it involves information that is publicly available and accessible to everyone on the team—regardless of their role in the process. Simply surveying the existing products and learning about their history, features, how they are used, and user opinions and ratings can be very beneficial to your own process moving forward.

- *Usability*: These aspects of research are regularly based upon three different areas: examining the usability issues that may be present in existing products, reviewing standard and current usability concerns in the industry, and making usability decisions for your own product. Usability research should be continuous throughout the UX Process. **Do not neglect considering accessibility issues within your research**.

- *Analytics*: Analytical research is often done only with existing conditions—since something must first exist to be analyzed. This form of research is often data-based and gathered through the measurement of behavior-based metrics. Because of this, such research is often more suitable for use further along in the UX Process but can still be performed even in early stages wherever measurable data points exist.

- *Observation*: Most usually accomplished in the form of user testing, observation is often considered while we are further along in the process—similar to analytics. You can observe users' experiences with the current version of your product following a release or can invite users to click through wireframes and prototypes as you move through the process. Again, this is also a good method for surfacing issues around accessibility.

Of course, no matter at which point of the entire process you are involved in at any given time, keep space for additional methods of research that may be useful during the current phase of your work or down the road in future aspects of the project lifecycle. Being too strict and rigid in handling research puts you at a disadvantage because you will be blinded to additional possibilities.

Think about your approach to research like a scientist should approach the scientific method. If a scientist considers a set of theories and hypotheses to be the unwavering truth, they will often not consider alternative research when presented with some new information that contradicts their beliefs. Scientific truths change all the time—take the concept of spontaneous generation as an example. The theory of spontaneous generation states that living creatures can emerge from nonliving matter. Such a belief was held as far back as Aristotle, and he even made reference to others who came before that held this same theory in one form or another.

A commonly cited example of spontaneous generation is that a pile of filthy rags left alone will eventually produce rats and bugs (Figure 2-4). Anyone could observe this "fact" and take it to be true that the rats were generated from the piles themselves and not through some other means. Why? Because no one bothered to perform any carefully monitored, continuous research into the matter.

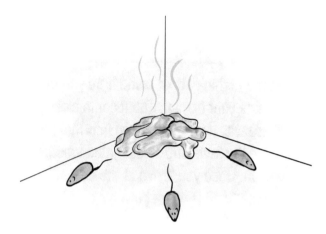

Figure 2-4. The theory of spontaneous generation was discredited in 1859 after being accepted by scientists for thousands of years—thanks to continuous research

We hold it to be true today that vermin and insects do not spontaneously generate from piles of old rags and garbage... but this was not the case even just 150 years ago! If Louis Pasteur and John Tyndall had not been open to, and actively involved in, new research, which went against the prevailing view... we might still hold the view that living creatures could be generated from nonliving matter.

Research as part of the UX Process should be just as continuous for us just as it should be in the realms of science. Who knows what commonly held scientific beliefs will be shown as nonsense over the next 100, 200, or even 500 years. Continuous research and more refined methods and tools are the key to greater understanding of the world we live in—and to better identifying and solving problems in our own work through the UX Process.

The data collected from later phases of the project can be just as important as what is initially gathered through research. New insights can help developers and other stakeholders understand whether they are on the right track or need to pivot in some way. It is sometimes difficult to make a drastic change later in the UX Process, but if the research shows such a change to be beneficial to the user experience... there really shouldn't be any debate around whether or not changes should be undertaken.

Tip   Take some time to think about some time you made the decision to re-evaluate your opinion about some closely held belief in your life. Likely, there was a formal or even informal research aspect while you questioned the facts and investigated whether alternative views held any weight. Once you arrive at the decision to adjust your viewpoint on some matter, it is almost always a difficult process— but that didn't deter you from making the necessary adjustments. Late-phase research in the UX Process can take the same form as personal viewpoint shifts—and is often a difficult thing. The important aspect that you should remember is that the difficulty in either scenario is worth the outcomes produced.

Considering our parking kiosk scheduling app example once more... perhaps toward the end of the development phase, research comes back to show that the way that the confirmation screen was designed is a stumbling block for test users. Changes are suggested, which involve the design team reworking much of that portion of the screen, and, of course, a number of adjustments have to be made by the development team as well—perhaps even the removal of a large portion of the code base for that section and additional, significant changes to back-end systems. What if the entire project release had to be delayed to address and correct these items discovered through continuous research? It is worth the pain and effort to rework, readjust, and rewrite the experience to conform to what the research shows is more ideal for your users.

Research and Systems Impact

As we have already mentioned, research done well should have a positive impact on any systems produced through the UX Process. The problems identified during the early research phase—both large and small—will drive the formation and direction of design systems and what systems are assembled by the development team as well. A continuous reflection of initial research along with the addition of new data acquired during subsequent research along the process will direct the overall plans and provide an active measure of success throughout the project's lifespan. The data gathered throughout the process can be compared to initial expectations as well—which is immensely beneficial once the project is complete and everyone reflects on the process.

In the previous section, we detailed how painful solving a larger problem can be when identified later in the project lifecycle. It doesn't necessarily need to happen that way, of course, though this possibility always exists. The most preferable outcome from the initial research phase would be to clearly identify both large and small problems that must be solved through design and development work (Figure 2-5) so that everything can be considered in an organic way from the very start. As a developer, you have an understanding of the back-end services, APIs, and databases that most stakeholders have honestly very little knowledge of. For this reason, it is very important that the development team is involved early within the research phase—even if only to be better informed as to what systems might be necessary for the functional elements of the product to operate.

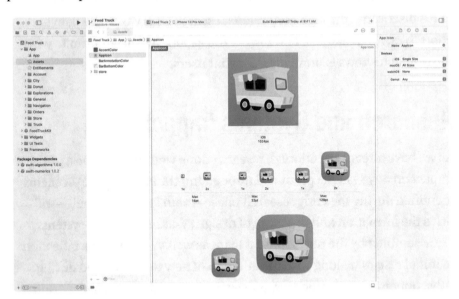

Figure 2-5. *The research data should direct which platform(s) should be targeted and the frameworks and technologies put into place to achieve our goals, in this case the design of the app icon for iOS. Image gathered from* `https://developer.apple.com/xcode/`

Implementing systems that can gather analytics is beneficial in the long term, as the data gathered can be compared to any expectations derived from the foundational research phase and will allow adjustments and pivots to be made when necessary. Remember: it is never a bad thing to respond to verified data in a meaningful way... but to not respond is just inviting problems down the road for everyone involved. This includes the user!

Artifacts and Deliverables

As a developer, you can make use of the results of this research phase to determine the course of action your team should take when building out the back-end systems and which platforms and technologies should be used for the experience. It is often helpful to build out a set of deliverables and assets based on the research data that can help guide everyone involved as you move ahead in the process. We get a lot deeper into this subject in Chapter 6, but this is a great place to introduce you to the concepts.

Deliverables at this phase of the process will often include the following:

- *Product goals statement*: Documentation that describes the overall vision for the project through a clear set of measurable goals. This sort of document can be used for planning but also in reflection along the way to keep everyone on target until the project is completed.

- *Research plan*: A living document that adapts to best conform to the data as it is gathered via the various research methods mentioned in this chapter. It is considered a living document because of the continuous nature of the research process and should change as the data dictates.

41

- *Competitive analysis*: An overview document that identifies competing products and explores both their strengths and weaknesses. This document can help determine what your team should focus on with your own product and even certain elements to avoid— based upon the user reaction to competing products.

- *Personas*: A persona (Figure 2-6) is a detailed description of a mythical individual target user for your product. By describing your various target users through different personas, you can gain a better understanding of the audience as a whole when making important decisions. Personas can take many forms but are normally standardized according to an individual project and lean heavily into demographics.

About:

Julia is an avid runner but often need to take her car into the city for groceries, appointments, and social events. She considers herself to ne patient but is often frustrated by poorly designed interactions.

Goals:

When visiting the city, Julia want to find available parking for her vehicle, park quickly and without delay

Frustrations:

Julia currently uses the physical kiosks as she does not trust the app Experience do confusing aspects of the Ui and being fined when she thought she had confirmed payment using the app but was mistaken.

Bio

Age: 27
Female
Single
College Graduate
Income: $55,000

Figure 2-6. *Personas based upon the findings from your research can assist all stakeholders involved in defining the problem. This one was created in Adobe XD using an image from the PhotoSplash plugin*

- *Research report*: A guide that documents and presents the totality of your foundational research to all product stakeholders in the organization. This report often contains many of the individual elements, as expressed previously, organized into a single, comprehensive document.

With a set of organized artifacts in place to help guide everyone through the upcoming phases of the project... all stakeholders should be clear as to the problem being solved, how the product can best solve this problem, and a path to begin planning the necessary steps to make this all a reality for the user. While every project may not benefit from these particular deliverables—or even associated artifacts we haven't mentioned in this chapter—having a diverse set of documents based upon solid research activities is fundamental to the success of your project moving forward.

Tip   You will collect a lot of data during the initial phase of UX research. The deliverables chosen and assembled should help clarify the findings from this set of data but should never include all the data gathered. Including too much data can make things confusing for other stakeholders and will muddy the focus of the product trajectory. Include in your deliverables only enough data to inform and clarify the research for all stakeholders—never anything more. The full set of data can still exist apart from any artifacts in case anyone needs to return to it down the road, but that is different from what should be formally presented to the team.

As we've outlined in this section, organizing the collection of data gathered during the UX research phase is incredibly important for communication within your organization. Producing a proper set of documents and artifacts can make the distribution of information as streamlined and accessible as possible to all team members. While UX researchers are primarily responsible for gathering this foundational data, having the involvement of designers and developers at this early stage is an important strategy for the organization as a whole—and should always be considered.

The Developer's Role in the Research Phase

In more traditional organizational scenarios, developers will not get involved in the product lifecycle until the last phases of the production. This most often occurs once the design team has completed their designs and prototypes and passes this information over to the development team through design systems, prototypes, generated code bundles, and other deliverables that can be interpreted and used by developers to create the functional product. We suggest a much different approach in this book— that developers should be included in even the initial phases of research expressed throughout this chapter in order to better interpret certain data points gathered and better guide the process of having a functional product that pleases the user.

As an example, what if during the foundational research phase it is discovered that the primary competitor product is only available on Apple iOS but that there is a massive clamoring from potential users requesting an Android version of the experience (Figure 2-7)? The UX research team would likely recognize this and recommend that the product being developed should include applications for both mobile platforms. How would that influence the designer's work that follows? What would be the eventual content and specifications passed along for development? It might be on point, or it could miss the mark on one platform or the other in spectacular ways without taking into account differences between both platforms.

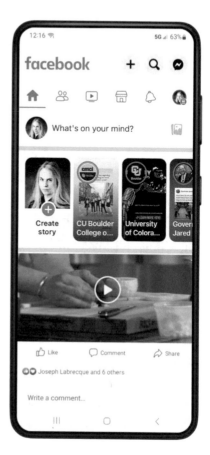

Figure 2-7. *The differences between platforms are often seen as surface-level such as the different video controllers... but developers know better and should be on-hand to influence and guide such decisions*

Designers would likely recognize certain differences and account for these within their prototypes and asset designs. There is certainly a large set of platform and back-end technical detail that only the developer can address. Not addressing such important aspects until that late into the process is a sure way to introduce costly issues that should have been addressed earlier. Including developers in every phase of the process can avoid such problems—if not eliminate them completely.

> **Tip**   As a developer, you can work to own that specialized role across all phases of the UX Process by communicating with all stakeholders early on. Dialog with the design team, the research team, and project management can increase the familiarity you all have with one another and the trust provided to each aspect of the organization. Contributing feedback, suggestions, and guidance early and often is a sure way to "sell" the benefits to your involvement with any project from conception to conclusion. Once others recognize the benefits of such collaboration… you'll no longer need to make the arguments for involvement as they will already be clear and present.

When developers have access to the initial research and can dialog with the research team early on, you can all work together in determining how the various functions necessary for solving a particular problem can best be implemented. With designers also involved in this early phase of the process, they can build a friendly rapport with the development team as well—which will greatly benefit the following phases of the process as understanding increases beyond design issues alone. There are really no drawbacks to including everyone's involvement and being open to such feedback and guidance in these early stages of the process.

Conclusion

In this chapter, we explored how to define the problem that our experience intends to solve for the user through the developer investing time in the research phase of the overall UX Process. We explored what UX research commonly entails and what the differences and benefits are between foundational and continuous research during the entire product design lifecycle. From a specifically developer-oriented perspective, we considered how this foundational research can impact decisions made around various platforms and systems to be considered and what artifacts and deliverables can be expected at this phase of the process. Finally, we considered the major benefits to including developers—and designers as well—in these early stages of the entire process.

Next, we'll expand upon the results of our initial research in determining the scope of our project and establishing the details of our minimum viable product (**MVP**) as we continue along the UX Process. We'll explore how to define the purpose of our product's existence and explore ways in which we can refine the focus and scope through tools such as a prioritization matrix and consideration of existing user behaviors.

CHAPTER 3

Determining the Scope and MVP

The minimum viable product is that version of a new product which allows a team to collect the maximum amount of validated learning about customers with the least effort.

—Eric Ries
https://www.startuplessonslearned.com/2009/08/
minimum-viable-product-guide.html
"Minimum Viable Product: A Guide"

Once our initial set of research is in place—having been collected, sorted, and delivered in an organized fashion—we can then make use of the findings from our research in *defining* the problem to begin planning how to *solve* the problem in continuing along with the UX Process. We begin solving the problem by determining the scope of features for the experience to be developed and what the minimum viable product (**MVP**) should encompass in order to plan a workable approach to design and development of the product.

In this chapter, we will focus on methods of determining the scope of our product with considerations toward defining what our MVP should encompass—in consideration for its overall reason to exist. We'll do so by breaking large tasks into smaller, modular, more manageable ideas and identify how our product can uniquely solve a problem for the user

© Tom Green and Joseph Labrecque 2023
T. Green and J. Labrecque, *A Guide to UX Design and Development*, Design Thinking,
https://doi.org/10.1007/978-1-4842-9576-2_3

and how our approach to this problem is unique in light of possible competition. We'll then look to define what features are high priority vs. those that are simply nice to have... or even may be a stumbling block to users. We'll wrap up with considerations for listening to the users of a product, staying on target, and avoiding feature creep as development progresses.

Why Scaling Our View Matters

When taking on any large project, it is often daunting to consider every aspect that must be addressed as an overall product. In fact, many people become paralyzed with inaction when presented with a task filled with complexities such as this. Just as how a full application is made up of many smaller screens and components, a major project should be tackled bit by bit while still keeping in mind the whole.

One of the best approaches to any major undertaking is to consider the smaller pieces and start building everything upward from these smaller, fundamental units (Figure 3-1). Even something like this book, for example, was written word-by-word... building paragraphs... sections... and chapters. Tackling massive projects by focusing on their smaller components is a great way to relieve the anxiety often associated with getting started and can often be very productive—as before you know it... the smaller pieces that have been addressed come together to form something much larger. Of course, this is not to say that you should ever lose sight of the larger project, but if it becomes overwhelming to the point of paralysis... remember to focus on the smaller pieces of the whole in order to progress.

Figure 3-1. *Focus on the smaller tasks and units when building something more grand—similar to how an assortment of blocks, stones, and bricks are used together in the formation of a larger, more functional building*

In addition to tackling any such problem in a way that scales down the view of the whole to make it more manageable, you might also consider approaching any urgent problems that must be solved in light of these small units. Problems can often be broken down into very precise pieces— and as you likely know very well from previous development work... many problems can be traced to a single character in your code that throws the entire program off. Developers know better than anyone that small problems in no way mean insignificant problems! This is why the best way to deal with complexity is to start with simplicity.

Tip   As an exercise, consider a time when you used this approach to help tackle a large project that wasn't related to your work as a developer or UX professional. Think back on the last time you had a project around the yard or the house that seemed a bit too large and perhaps even quite daunting when initially approached. How did you make decisions around your approach? Were you able to tackle the overall project by focusing on one aspect at a time in the way we've discussed? These tactics are universal!

Let's take use development project as an example of this. In the following figure (Figure 3-2), we see the results of a program being run— which throws an exception that completely breaks the entire experience for the user. Looking at the big picture, any user... and likely even some developers... may throw their hands up in frustration and become overwhelmed with the entire program. When the code is examined at a finer level, however, paying attention to smaller units of lines and characters in the code... the problem *and the solution* become apparent.

Figure 3-2. *Even the smallest problem in your code can render the entire program useless*

Not only is the program-crashing problem easily fixable but using tools like a debugger often will tell us exactly what the problem is so that we understand the remedy as well. Reducing our view into these smaller units within the scope of the UX Process is a similar way to troubleshoot the problems we face—and when defining the larger scope of the product, there are often tools and workflows that can guide us to the best decisions, similar to the function of a debugger or other developer tools.

Product Purpose and Reason to Exist

Though the problem has been successfully defined as part of the UX research phase, and before we turn our attention to the features our product should include, we should spend some time asking the big questions. For instance, why are we even going through all of this? What significant differences might there be between our product and any competing, or similar, products in scope and function? Most importantly... what is the reason our product should even exist at all? At this point in the process, if you cannot clearly communicate why the product is being considered, you probably shouldn't even be considering moving ahead in the process. If your team is having some difficulty with these questions, identifying the overall purpose should help clarify what you are all attempting and why.

Tip   If you cannot clearly define the purpose for your product, it may not be worth exploring any further. Switch gears and find another problem to solve that can better benefit users and help the team create an elevated experience everyone can feel empowered by.

Given what we have learned from our research, consider... based upon that data... what your product can provide the user that is lacking in similar experiences or competing products. If a product exists for the purpose of serving the user (Figure 3-3), consider how your particular feature set will provide some benefit over what already may exist in the market. The features that set your product apart from the rest are the ones that can serve the user best but also fulfill obligations to the greater team and organization.

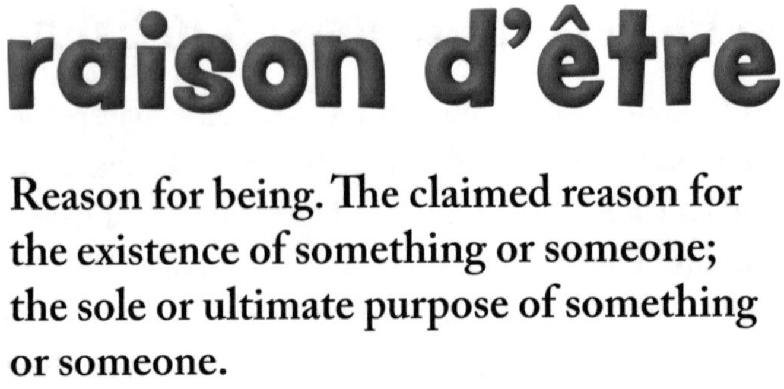

raison d'être

Reason for being. The claimed reason for the existence of something or someone; the sole or ultimate purpose of something or someone.

Figure 3-3. *One of the most important tasks at this phase is to establish the raison d'être for your product*

If you can successfully define the product purpose, you are well on the way to determining the raison d'être for your product. While the purpose and reason to exist may seem similar at first, they can actually be considered as different—yet related—aspects of the product:

- *Product purpose*: Describes the functional aspects of your product and how they contribute to solving the problem, as defined through UX research. A fine-grained declaration that details how the product operates and why.

- *Raison d'être*: A more general definition that describes why users need the product in a general way without relying upon any references to technical aspects or individual features. How does the product impact the lives of its users?

Take the Instagram mobile app, for example. The product purpose would be to allow users to take photographs, apply filters and edits, and then share the photographs with other users. The raison d'être though… might be considered something along the lines of empowering users to connect with one another through photography. The main point—*and ultimate end*—is the same… just expressed through different contexts. One is product-focused and the other is user-focused.

Enduring Value in the Minimum Viable Product

Determining what features are included in the minimum viable product is important for a number of reasons (Figure 3-4). For one thing, it defines an outline for your team to work with when designing the experience and further brings it to life through development. As we explained earlier in this chapter, it is always a good idea to start with the smaller components to define the whole. By figuring out what your MVP should consist of early on, you are doing just that! Another reason for the importance of the MVP is it backs up the raison d'être and helps communicate ideas about the experience you are building in a more tangible, feature-by-feature way. This also allows you to focus on the core features of the product you are building. Sticking to the heart of your product—the MVP—will serve to keep everyone on the same page and help avoid any sort of feature creep down the line.

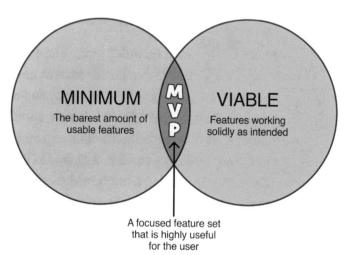

Figure 3-4. *The minimum viable product is focused on specific features that are highly useful to your core product audience*

The MVP itself should express a number of things about your product, which, by themselves, would be incomplete. What you are looking for when defining the MVP is an experience for the user that contains a core set of features that are both focused and simple for the user to understand and make use of... but also are rational and work in a meaningful way. Figuring out which specific features simultaneously fulfill these needs will help the team arrive at the definition of your MVP and guide all stakeholders to a path forward along the UX Process.

Tip   When considering what the MVP for your product should entail, a good exercise is to think of an existing experience or product you are well-acquainted with and try to decipher what the teams that built this product have defined as their MVP feature set. It can also be helpful to try and identify features that you see as standing apart from what could be the established MVP for the chosen product. The raison d'être can also provide guidelines to the MVP.

While sticking with the core MVP is incredibly important when building your experience, know the MVP can be adjusted as new features are requested by users or if certain aspects of the product need to be adjusted for any reason. Any changes to the MVP, however, should always retain those dual aspects of being both *minimal* and *viable* into consideration before being accepted as part of an adjusted MVP definition. All too often, the MVP is ignored following a product launch as new features are added without considering these aspects and how they might fit within your accepted MVP definition.

Determining the Minimum Viable Product

Deciding upon both the product purpose and overall raison d'être can assist you in defining the scope of your project and determining what the minimum viable product (MVP) should entail. There are two main concerns when determining the MVP of your design: the features most important for the user and those that are important to your team. Of course, if these features overlap, all the better.

- **What is important for the user?**

  The user of your product desires to launch the parking app, enter the necessary information to secure a parking spot, easily pay the charge, and be ensured that they are safe from any fines when the process concludes.

- **What is important for the team?**

  The team aims to increase user adoption of the product and to reduce the number of user complaints and problems present to ensure continued usage.

Tip   Taking our parking payment app into consideration once more… what do you think the MVP might consist of? What potential features might be secondary to the core MVP? How might those extra features benefit or detract from those that are core to the experience?

One of the most-used methods of determining what features should be included in your minimum viable product definition based on the data gathered from the UX research phase is the prioritization matrix. This is a simple tool that takes the form of four quadrants (Figure 3-5).

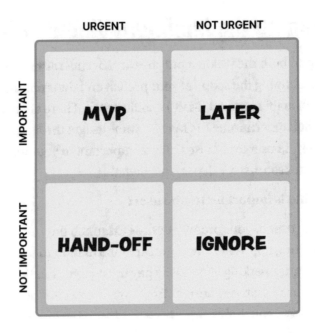

Figure 3-5. *Example of an Eisenhower-style prioritization matrix to determine MVP features*

Features derived from our research are plotted across this matrix and evaluated based upon which quadrant they are assigned to. The team decides, based upon aspects of importance and urgency, and likely amid a great deal of discussion, into which quadrant each feature should fall:

- *Important/Urgent*: These tasks or features should be tackled immediately as they are integral to the product success, and timeline is a factor.

- *Important/Not Urgent*: These tasks or features are integral to the product success but can be scheduled for later. Often, if this is a product feature, it relies upon other features that need to be put in place first and so is not as urgent simply due to that fact.

- *Not Important/Urgent*: These tasks and features can often be delegated or assigned to others. Perhaps there are new members of the team or even interns that can handle these items. Delegating these timely—yet unimportant—tasks can free you and your team to tackle the most important and urgent items.

- *Not Important/Not Urgent*: If anything falls within this quadrant, it should be dismissed. No one should be wasting time or energy on tasks and features that are not important or urgent.

The prioritization matrix is editorial in nature. The team should never be fearful of casting certain features aside if these activities warrant it. The matrix can be used to distill the set of defined features and tasks into certain groups to define the minimum viable product and, moving forward, what could be considered as secondary features, what tasks or features can be handed off to another team to handle, and, very importantly… which features should no longer be considered for inclusion.

Note   This type of prioritization matrix is often called an Eisenhower matrix due to US president Dwight Eisenhower making abundant use of it as a time management tool during his various roles in the US Army and NATO and even as president. Going along with and confirming this practice, Eisenhower famously stated, "I have two kinds of problems, the urgent and the important. The urgent are not important, and the important are never urgent."

Over the years, a number of variations of the prioritization matrix have been developed. You may see examples that factor in additional dimensions such as how time-consuming a certain task might be or how much effort would be involved to complete a task. No matter how your features are plotted and aligned, any use of such a matrix can help a great deal when trying to discern what exactly your minimum viable product should feature.

Generate New Ideas Grounded in User Behaviors

New features may be introduced—which go beyond the minimum viable product definition—at any time during the UX Process. This can often even occur during the post-launch phase when considering feature-bearing updates as the product becomes more widely adopted. No matter where we are in the process, the team must keep in mind how users interact with the product—and how additional features may possibly weaken the MVP.

Oftentimes, as developers, we think that more features equal more options for the user and thus make for a more appealing product for the user. This is not always true, though, as adding features the user never asked for or ignores completely can add complexity to the user interface and complicate what was once a simple and joyful experience into something that feels more like a chore (Figure 3-6).

Figure 3-6. *Many users see the Instagram mobile app as a good example of feature creep—going from a laser-focused photo-centric tool in 2013 to adding on a number of distracting features like a store, Facebook Messenger, stories, and more…*

One of your authors uses the example of Instagram in his class. Instagram launched with a very focused, clear MVP, which users adored. It allowed anyone to share photos with friends and view their friends' photos. Pure and simple! Over the years, Instagram has added all sorts of features to the product, which dilute the original, core experience and make the product less friendly for users. It now includes a shop, a short-form video experience, integration with messaging apps, a convoluted feed algorithm, and much more that original users never wanted.

Tip   Whether a new product or an existing one with thousands of users, be careful of feature creep and how much you deviate from your defined MVP.

One of your authors used to work as a software engineer among a small team of talented designers, developers, and user-facing stakeholders at a well-known, private university. We built many products over a span of nearly two decades, but the one with the greatest user-base was a web application that enabled users to design and publish their professional portfolios. With thousands upon thousands of active users and an engaged community through which we were constantly receiving feedback and feature requests... it was very easy to fumble sometimes when deciding whether to build out a feature or not.

This web-based product (Figure 3-7), being so heavily user-facing, required a lot of collaboration between the development team and other stakeholders in the organization—especially once it became a mature, community-integrated product. At one point, we were approached by a very enthusiastic group of users who were interested in a way to link user portfolios in a more social way than was currently available. With such excitement and dedication from this group of users, we did build out the feature, "University Networking," and made it available to everyone.

University Networking

University Networking provides a mechanism for portfolio users to select areas of interest for display on their personal portfolios. This enables members of the university community with similar interests to identify and contact one another.

Manage University Networking Selections

1. Click on the University Networking button accessed from any page in your portfolio.

2. Click on Manage University Networking Selections.

3. Click on the title in which you would like to network (Countries of Origin, Sports, etc.) and check the specific category in which you are interested. Note: Multiple categories can be selected.

4. Click Submit.

Figure 3-7. *Even with documentation, feature creep can still appear as an unwanted distraction to users*

Note   The preceding screen is a fictional screen cap used by the university to familiarize users with UI. Maria Garcia does not exist.

Unfortunately, we didn't do our research, and it turns out a small group of users was very happy with the feature that resulted from our discussions... but the majority of our users were confused by an addition to the product that they mostly deemed useless and even confusing. The problem is that it diluted the core experience and went too far beyond our established *raison d'être* with the result being full-on feature creep.

Tip   No matter how good a feature request or new idea might seem, initially... it is always worth the effort to perform additional research to ensure that it will result in a positive experience for your users.

As a result of this, we knew that how we communicated with our users needed to be adjusted in order to keep such feature creep at bay while still enlivening the feedback loop that we had nurtured and grown over the years. Not only was it necessary to bring someone on board who could best interface with our users to perform research and analytics to bring back to the larger team... but it was also helpful to keep everyone focused on their own particular roles while keeping everyone who was invested, un-siloed and in communication around different aspects with each release cycle.

The best way to avoid this sort of feature creep and stay true to your MVP is to keep communication open between all stakeholders—but especially with your users and with the UX research team, as they should be conducting continual research throughout the lifetime of the product. In later chapters, we'll examine user testing—as this can be incredibly helpful when making such important decisions.

Conclusion

In this chapter, we've moved on from the UX research phase and have begun the task of determining the scope of our product and what features should be included and have developed a minimum viable product definition to steer us in our journey.

We began the chapter by considering our view of the tasks before us and how an approach that takes on smaller units to build into something greater can be a beneficial workflow—especially during this phase of the project. Before moving on, of course, we must define what exactly will be designed and developed—and included in any wireframes of prototypes. We learned that in order to achieve this understanding—in a general way—the reason your product should exist along with defining the product purpose is key to successfully moving along to other aspects of the process. We considered what the MVP should entail and why it is important to establish a set of features that include both aspects of importance and urgency. We wrapped up with considerations for listening to the users of a product, staying on target, and avoiding feature creep as design and development work progresses.

In the next chapter, we'll have a look at one of the most important items in the entire UX Process—the prototype—as we explore an examination of considerations around prototyping and the variety of stages within the prototyping process.

CHAPTER 4

The Prototype

It is the prototype that brings to life the "experience" behind "User Experience."

—Jerry Cao, UXPin
"The Ultimate Guide to Prototyping"

Nothing does more to bring a project to life than a prototype. Prototyping is the core of the creative process requiring both a highly developed sense of creativity and practicality. While wireframes may sketch out the basic blueprint and flow and mockups present the look and feel of the design, it is the prototype that either helps or hinders the user experience mission because you won't know if your ideas are valid until a user picks up a mouse and clicks an object or taps on the screen. At this point, the prototype becomes a "proof of concept" that will expose any usability or accessibility flaws behind the wireframes and mockups.

Before we dig into a deeper discussion of this subject, you need to know that anything can be a prototype. There is a misconception out there that a prototype is an entire project. You can thank such tools as Adobe XD, Figma, UXPin, and other tools for that one because the companies behind them have done very little, if anything, to dispel this myth.

Here's an example of how anything can be a prototype. The designer has pulled together a Submit button, and you have lightly coded the state changes. That button is a prototype and can be sent out to the team for comment and/or sent out for user testing. As the comments and test

© Tom Green and Joseph Labrecque 2023
T. Green and J. Labrecque, *A Guide to UX Design and Development*, Design Thinking,
https://doi.org/10.1007/978-1-4842-9576-2_4

results come in, the button will most likely undergo several iterations to get it right. Once that happens that button can be added to the design system and reused throughout the project. Bottom line? Prototyping gives you something to test with your users that enables you to iterate accurately.

In the long run, prototyping something as mundane as a button will make you more efficient. It is easier to make these changes now than to discover the usability and accessibility flaws later in the process.

Why Prototype?

Let's start this discussion with a question. Would you buy a pair of shoes without first trying them on? It only makes sense that users and the team test the project or hypothesis before the project lands in your team's lap.

Back in 2009, Todd Warfel literally wrote the Prototyping Bible in his book *Prototyping: A Practitioners Guide* (`https://rosenfeldmedia.com/books/prototyping`). According to Todd, there are several very valid reasons behind a decision to prototype. Among them are

> *Communication and collaboration*: It is very easy for a designer to say, "When the user clicks the Submit button, an overlay appears where the user can choose how long to park." This is where problems start. Everyone who hears it has a different idea of what the button looks like, what the overlay looks like, and even how fast it appears. From your perspective as the developer, the Compass of Blame starts swinging toward you because everyone imagined a different interaction. Prototype it and everyone is working from the same place because they can see and feel what the designer was saying. Even more important, the connection between the developers and the designers is established.

Freedom to fail: That may sound a bit harsh, but prototyping gives everyone the opportunity to see what works and what doesn't work. From that, they learn why it worked or didn't work, and that lesson is invaluable.

Sells the concept: When it comes to the stakeholders and the development team, a prototype makes for a killer pitch deck. They all get to "kick the tires" and get a deeper understanding of the project's intent than is gained from mockups and wireframes.

Tests usability: The user tests a prototype, and any issues that appear can be fixed before they get locked in with code. Studies show there is a roughly 25% reduction in post-release bugs when a prototype is involved.

There is no correct approach to prototyping. It is up to the team to decide what, when, and how to create prototypes, and this should be done at the start of the project rather than making decisions as you go along. If there is a prototyping application to be used, it, too, needs to be established at the start, and that decision involves which tool and its features are best suited to the scope and complexity of the project, not some personal preference.

Finally, you, as the developer, must be involved in these initial discussions. Not only will it allow you to become familiar with the project's intent but also the opportunity to start planning both the front-end and back-end system needs.

Accessibility First

When it comes to prototyping, one major aspect of the process that gets overlooked is accessibility. It is more than an <alt> tag, video captions, or access to screen readers. It deals with your users, whoever they are and wherever they may be, who will use the application or visit the website. You have absolutely no control over their health, potential disability, or even the situation in which they may be using your work.

Accessibility and inclusion should be rolled into the user research, which could examine potential visual, hearing, motor, and cognitive impairments that would be reflected in the personas or user stories the research generates.

Accessibility is not confined to a group of users with some specific abilities; it includes anyone experiencing any permanent, temporary, or situational disability. How would someone with one arm access the parking app? That's a permanent condition that should be addressed. How would a person whose arm is in a cast access the parking app? That is a temporary condition. How would someone carrying a briefcase or bag in one hand access the parking app? That is a situational condition. The common thread here is the app is being used with only one hand. Thus, accessibility shouldn't focus on specifics. Instead, the question to be asked by both the designers and the developers is: How do we make the content more usable and accessible to a general audience?

This topic is vast and well out of the scope of this book, but prototyping is where accessibility must be a prime goal, not an afterthought. The advantage for you is prototyping is an iterative process that moves the project to its MVP state. At each stage and even iteration of the process, the achievement of your accessibility and inclusion goals should be front and center. The last thing you need is to have someone ask about this topic when the high-fidelity prototype is out for testing.

Here are some guidelines from the Web Content Accessibility Guidelines (WCAG) to keep in mind as prototypes come into focus:

- Don't use links that read "Click Here" or are even more general such as "More." This addresses users with motor impairments, cognitive limitations, or visual disabilities and helps them use fewer keystrokes.

- Don't color-code information. Instead, use a combination of color text and shapes instead. This is especially important to users who have visual impairments such as color blindness or who use a monochrome monitor.

- The functionality of all UI components must be consistent. This is easily accomplished using a design system, component library, GitHub repository, or style guide. Again, people with a visual impairment benefit from this because the experience is both predictable and consistent.

- Don't rely on device-dependent interactions. If a component contains a hover state, for example, design that state so users can perceive the additional content and dismiss it without disrupting the experience. Users with low vision or cognitive disabilities may need that extra time to view the hover state's content with less distraction.

- Touch targets should be at least 9 mm square and are to be independent of the screen size, device, or resolution. Also, make sure there is enough negative space around controls to avoid having them interact with each other. This will benefit users with mobility issues such as hand tremors or who are in situations where only one hand can be used.

As we said, address accessibility first before you get deep into the prototyping process. If your team has the resources, seriously consider retaining the services of a web accessibility practitioner.

Tip   There are several resources out there, but one that would be most useful to both designers and developers is the WCAG 2.1. It can be found at `www.w3.org/WAI/WCAG21/Understanding/`. This is a comprehensive listing of the guidelines complete with descriptions, benefits, and examples for each guideline.

Another great resource is the Microsoft Inclusive Design site. It can be found at `www.microsoft.com/design/inclusive/` (Figure 4-1). Again, it is an excellent source for guidance around Inclusive Design, which they state right at the start:

Inclusive Design is a methodology, born out of digital environments, that enables and draws on the full range of human diversity. Most importantly, this means including and learning from people with a range of perspectives.

Recognize exclusion	Solve for one, extend to many	Learn from diversity
Designing for inclusivity not only opens up our products and services to more people, it also reflects how people really are. All humans grow and adapt to the world around them and we want our designs to reflect that.	Everyone has abilities, and limits to those abilities. Designing for people with permanent disabilities actually results in designs that benefit people universally. Constraints are a beautiful thing.	Human beings are the real experts in adapting to diversity. Inclusive design puts people in the center from the very start of the process, and those fresh, diverse perspectives are the key to true insight.

Figure 4-1. *Microsoft Inclusive Design*

The Current State of Prototyping

Unlike a race that starts when the gun sounds or the light turns green, when and how to prototype is up for debate. The traditional linear process looks something like this:

- *Sketching*: Break out the paper, pencils, markers, and whiteboards and start brainstorming.

- *Wireframing*: Using boxes, arrows, and squiggles, the underlying architecture is put into place.

- *Mockups*: The wireframes become detailed with the addition of color, typography, photos, and other visual details.

- *Interactivity*: The mockups are stitched together with the addition of light coding or the inclusion of animations and interactions to add more detail.

- *Development*: The project is handed to you for coding in the appropriate language to turn the prototype into the final product.

The choice of the word "traditional" is deliberate. With the arrival of Lean UX, rapid prototyping, Agile, and even a school of thought that advocates for coding as soon as possible, that traditional way of doing things is becoming outdated. Even so, prototyping is an incremental and iterative process that refines the screens to meet or test the hypothesis, as illustrated in Figure 4-2. Now would be a good time to look at a few of them.

Prototyping

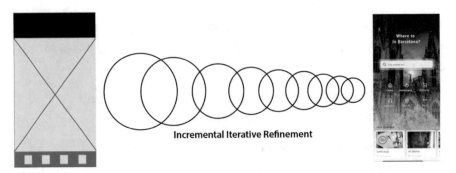

Figure 4-2. *Prototyping is an incremental iterative process*

Lean UX

The core concept behind this method is a prototype is the shortest space between you and your code (Figure 4-2). In short, skip steps and get right to the prototype. This may sound a bit odd, but there are definite advantages:

- *Time*: Skipping and/or consolidating the phases gets you to the end product a lot faster. That is true, but there is a very real risk of sacrificing quality along the way.

- *Efficiency*: By concentrating on only the essentials, the amount of time spent on nonessential tasks is minimized.

- *Experience*: Deliverables take a back seat to the prototype. The team's focus is on the user experience, not on who gets what and when. Pull the team together, state the design vision, and start iterating.

An example would be starting with a few rough sketches moving straight from the wireframes to the prototype by adding light interactions, screen transitions, and basic interactivity to the prototype. That prototype is sent out for a quick user test and iterating and testing as often as needed.

Rapid Prototyping

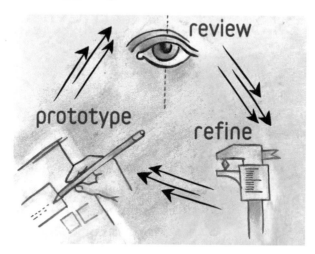

Figure 4-3. *Rapid prototyping process (source:* www.smashingmagazine.com/2010/06/design-better-faster-with-rapid-prototyping/*)*

Don't make the mistake of regarding this as a stand-alone process or one that morphs into the final solution. It is a messy process because rapid prototyping is all about quickly iterating based on feedback but is a tremendous way of helping the team to visualize the design and to find the path to the final product. Though rapid prototyping is a fundamental principle of Lean UX, it can be applied to any of the traditional steps presented earlier. One big fan of rapid prototyping is Lyndon Cerejo, UX strategist and UX lead for Capgemini, an international consulting company, who outlined the rapid prototyping process in a brilliant article for *Smashing Magazine*. According to Lyndon, the steps involving multiple iterations are

- *Prototype*: Convert the users' description of the solution into mockups, factoring in user experience standards and best practices. These descriptions can be drawn from personas and use cases.

- *Review*: Share the prototype with users and evaluate whether it meets their needs and expectations.

- *Refine*: Based on feedback, identify areas that need to be refined or further defined and clarified.

Straight to Code

It is a given that the shortest distance between two points is a straight line. It only makes sense, therefore, that going straight from prototype to code is also efficient. Let's be clear on one factor regarding this assumption: it only works with a clear plan of attack. Introduce code early into the design process, and the development process is built from a solid foundation, which implies fewer code revisions.

If this approach appeals to you, then you need to start with a paper sketch, paper prototype, or digital wireframe and then dive into the HTML or another language you may choose depending on the desired target platforms. By starting with paper or a whiteboard, concepts and approaches can be fully explored and either accepted or rejected. Avoid this step, and you run the real risk of producing a bland concept because the code locks it in.

Finally, you need to insist on being involved in this process right from the start. The last thing you need is for the development team to see the prototype sketches for the first time accompanied by a long list of instructions.

Tip   There are a lot of digital tools available for creating paper prototypes or wireframes that you can work from. Sneekpeekit.com has a number of templates for paper prototypes, and Miro, Figma, UXPin, and Adobe XD have whiteboards or plugins that can be used for wireframes.

Agile and Prototyping

Agile and UX don't always play well together. The reason being was Agile never accounted for UX design. While the importance of UX has grown exponentially over the past few years, many companies still find it challenging to mesh UX design and Agile workflows together. Yet the compelling need to accomplish this is evident:

In the 2021 Annual State of Agile Report, the report's authors state Agile adoption within software development teams increased from 37% in 2020 to 87% in 2021.

Almost half of the respondents said there were significant increases in the business value delivered and customer/user satisfaction.

The Scrum methodology was the most popular Agile technique.

Broad organizational recognition and acceptance of DevOps continues to grow. In the survey, 75% of respondents indicate DevOps is important or very important to their organization with only 9% stating it has no importance.

Figure 4-4. *State of Agile Report (source: https://digital.ai/ resource-center/analyst-reports/state-of-agile-report)*

As you may have guessed, Agile works well in a rapid prototyping environment because the bits and pieces of the experience are designed, wired up, tested, and iterated upon regularly. Even so, there is a tendency to confuse a rapid prototype with an MVP. A rapid prototype is a step toward the minimum viable product because the MVP is a stand-alone product that has been coded up and is ready for launch. The rapid prototype focuses more on design than code and is not a viable product on its own.

If this is more of a design step than a development step, then where does the developer fit in? To answer that question, let's look at our hypothetical parking app.

There is a screen where the user will be asked to input their license plate number. The odds are pretty good in a rapid prototyping environment that element will become a component, but before then it will undergo several design changes around whether there should be a border around the input field and what color the border will be, the size of the field, the font used, and so on.

What won't iterate is the data being input into the license plate field. While all of this is going on, you can turn your attention to how that data will be used, stored, and checked. Your front-end developer will also get a good look at the element's function by introspecting the code generated by a prototyping application or being tasked with writing the HTML or other code that adds the light functionality while at the same time determining how the data will be passed to the back end.

As the various iterations move through the process to the final state, the task of connecting the data from the front end to the back end becomes easier because the back-end data processes have been put in place. By building up to the final product, improvements can be made at a rapid pace, which also has one significant benefit for you: it avoids changes once the product is released into the wild.

What to Prototype?

Knowing the various prototyping methodologies is good, but the basic question you may be asking is, "What gets prototyped?" At the risk of being facetious, the answer is, as stated earlier: *Anything can be a prototype.*

It all comes down to fidelity, and that depends on how low-, medium-, or high-fidelity visuals (detail) and functionality are combined. For those unfamiliar with the term "fidelity," it has everything to do with detail. Low fidelity could be something like a wireframe, a box on a screen, or a paper prototype. Medium fidelity could be the screens in a click-thru prototype, and a high-fidelity prototype is close to the MVP with the functionality in place. With that out of the way, let's look at how functionality and detail relate to each other when it comes to creating a prototype.

Low Detail, Low Functionality

The value proposition here is simple. They cost nothing to produce, are easy to create, and are disposable. For example, a paper prototype for one of the parking app's screens is quick to make and has zero or little functionality, but what it does is put something in the team's hands that can highlight structural issues. By iterating the paper prototype... the UX hypothesis can be proven or disproven, features can be easily added or removed, and the flow can start to be established. Along the way, you will be able to refine and solidify the feature set based on user needs exposed during the research phase. Just be aware interactivity issues can't be addressed unless you regard sliding another piece of paper into the template, touching a drawing, or lifting a Post-It note as interactivity.

One final piece of advice: Start with mobile (Figure 4-5). Do this and you are forced to prioritize content, thanks to the limited screen real estate along with considerations for touch. Do this and it becomes much easier to scale up to tablets and web pages than were you to start with a desktop version and work your way down to a mobile device. This will also keep you, the developer, happy in you can start planning both the front-end development and the back end.

Figure 4-5. *A typical low detail–low functionality prototype*

Tip   Though this method stresses paper, one of the authors has also advocated that digital prototyping applications can be used instead. He calls it a "content wireframe" (Figure 4-6). Instead of jumping into the boxes and arrows commonly used in wireframing, you first block out the space for the content. In this way, you not only turn your focus away from the design elements (the content), but this approach makes starting with mobile much easier to accomplish. By creating this super low-fidelity wireframe… the focus is on establishing content placement, flow, and hierarchy before the big gray boxes are replaced with boxes and arrows.

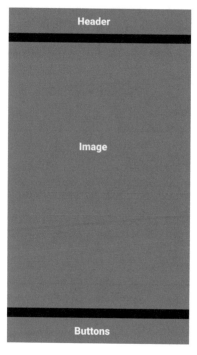

Figure 4-6. *Content wireframes are all about "blocking" out sections of the page so you can start to visualize how much space is required for each category of content*

Low Detail, High Functionality

These prototypes (Figure 4-7) are either created in some sort of prototyping software or handed over to the front-end team for production. Regardless of which way is chosen, these things are more like interactive wireframes than anything else.

Figure 4-7. *Using software, light functionality can be added to a prototype*

Though you may be thinking, "Why bother?", these prototypes can set the foundation for the interaction design and can be subjected to user testing, thanks to their light functionality. They are also a great way of further testing the hypothesis, and, for the stakeholders, this will be the opportunity to "kick the tires" and get a sense of what the project may look like and how it will work. As a developer, the advantage to you is it is a dandy replacement for a ton of formal documentation.

What makes this prototype approach so appealing is its lack of detail. They are vague enough that feedback will be more to the point yet have enough functionality to explore user flows. On top of that, this approach is ideal for a Lean process. The interactivity can be explored and tested without the distraction of visual elements such as color palettes, typeface pairing, images, and so on, which can be done later in Photoshop, Sketch, or other drawing and imaging applications.

High Detail, Low Functionality

This method, in many respects, can be regarded as an interactive mockup—which is nothing more than a click-through using hot spots on the screen (Figure 4-8). Going right to this prototype without starting with paper or a content wireframe is dangerous. They validate your hypothesis because they have been explored and iterated with a focus on the information architecture and content structure. This prototype focuses on visual design aspects other than core interactions... which can be quite expensive to address at a later date.

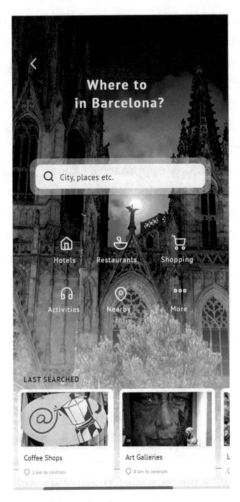

Figure 4-8. *Screens from Photoshop or Sketch can be used for click-through prototypes*

Getting to this step is rather easy because a screen designed in, say... Photoshop or Sketch can be easily dropped into a prototyping application. If the low-detail prototype was created in a prototyping application, all the boxes and arrows from that prototype could be replaced with the assets from Photoshop or Sketch.

Finally, this prototype serves all the purposes of a mockup—the visual design is in place, the stakeholders get a first glimpse of the user interface, the concept is presented to the clients, etc.—along with limited interactivity.

From a developer's point of view, you are getting a first look at the assets that will eventually be handed to you. This would be a good time to sit down with the designers and start laying out the content specifications. This will include such things as image resolution for iOS and Android devices and whether vector images should also have the resulting Scalable Vector Graphics (SVG) code accompanying them.

Tip   When creating the hot spots, follow what we call the "Fat Finger" rule. If the click-through is to be shown on a phone, tablet, or another touch-enabled device, make the hot spot a minimum of 40–50 pixels square. You have no control over how fat someone's fingers can be, and small hot spots most likely won't work. At the suggested dimension, you will be able to accommodate practically the size of any fingertip touching the screen.

High Detail, High Functionality

This prototype (Figure 4-9) is as close to the final product as you can get and can be either produced through prototyping applications or hand-coded by the front-end team. With complete visuals and functionality, this prototype is ideal for user testing and circulation to the team for feedback because it can act as a "living technical spec" for both the designers and developers.

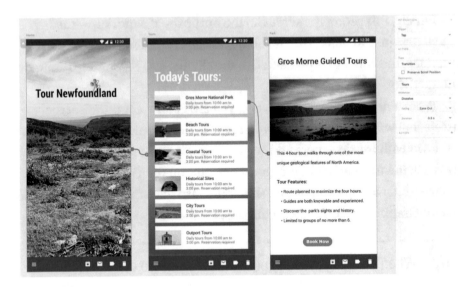

Figure 4-9. *Interactive prototype in Adobe XD*

At this point… the assets should all be in their proper format, the design system should be in place, and the back-end team has documented how the data passed from the application or website will be handled. This last point is important. A prototype typically doesn't accept data or make demands on any systems being developed. Though clients may assume this prototype is the final product, they would be making a bad assumption.

This prototype, if subjected to user testing and feedback from the stakeholders, will most likely require several "tweaks." This is not the time to make major changes, which is why we use the word "tweaks." Anything requiring a major change should have been caught and addressed in the high detail–low functionality prototype.

Conclusion

As you have discovered… prototyping involves more than kicking out the full interactive prototype and shooting it out for feedback and user testing. It is a methodical process that refines the hypothesis and brings it to life through an iterative process. It is also a process that gets underway during the research process as accessibility and inclusion issues are identified and addressed. We looked at several prototyping approaches and methods, which should give you a solid understanding of what needs to be done and the developer's role in the process.

A key takeaway from this chapter should be that anything can be a prototype, which can then be sent out for review and testing. Most of all, prototyping is how you, the developer, get an insight into the design team's "intent" by seeing it rather than having it described to you or included in some form of documentation.

CHAPTER 5

The Design System Library

A design system is your single source of truth.

—Marcin Treder
Former CEO, UXPin

Over the past couple of years, the concept of Design Systems has moved to the forefront of the UX conversation. This is quite understandable. With the rise of apps and websites, whether at the enterprise or personal level, the experience must be consistent from the first pixel to the last pixel and from the first screen to the last screen. It has to be that way because their only competitive advantage is the "experience." Product features and ratings may sell the app or website, but it is the experience that will keep the people who have downloaded or visited it, recognizing its value and regularly using it. The result is an incredible amount of pressure on UX teams to keep the experience consistent and to work faster. That is a recipe for chaos. Design does not easily scale, and the demand for more efficient and productive workflows, though understandable, puts enormous pressure on the UX team to do more in less time.

© Tom Green and Joseph Labrecque 2023
T. Green and J. Labrecque, *A Guide to UX Design and Development*, Design Thinking,
https://doi.org/10.1007/978-1-4842-9576-2_5

In many respects this has sparked a UX hiring boom, yet scaling through hiring is nothing more than a myth if there are no standards in place. Every new hire will most likely bring new color ideas, new typography suggestions, and new design patterns or other influences to the project. Add all of this to the mix and inconsistency takes hold, not to mention the eventual increase in maintenance costs. It's a lot like entropy in physics where all systems move to a state of disorder.

This brings us to the subject of this chapter: design systems impose order on potential disorder. Start the process of gradually growing a design system, and the entropy risk and design inconsistency decline along with a corresponding increase in the speed of software development. The takeaway? Design does indeed scale. But it only scales when a design system is in place.

Before we start you need to understand a design system is a lot more than a pattern library or some other document. A design system is a blueprint for product development. It documents all of the design fundamentals, visual assets, and patterns. Also, all code references are included for each element in the design system. In this way, design scales right alongside development. A change in one aspect ripples through the others, and all changes are instantly applied to each instance of that change in the prototype.

The Single Source of Truth

As a product team grows, its processes become more difficult to manage. Without some sort of standardized workflow or toolkit in place, there is a real risk that the team's inefficiencies and inconsistencies will have a negative result on the product. Large organizations such as Salesforce and Airbnb came to this realization very early in the game and did something about it. Karri Saarinen, principal designer and creator of the Airbnb design system, explained why in his article "Building a Visual Language" in which he outlined the creation of Airbnb's design system when he wrote

Design has always been largely about systems, and how to create products in a scalable and repeatable way. From Pantone colors to Philips screws, these systems enable us to manage the chaos and create better products. Digital products are perhaps the most fertile ground for implementing these systems and yet it's not often considered a priority.

A unified design system is essential to building better and faster; better because a cohesive experience is more easily understood by our users, and faster because it gives us a common language to work with.

```
—https://airbnb.design/
building-a-visual-language/
```

The need for a common language is driven by some common factors. Among them are

- *Inconsistencies across products and platforms*: Introduce inconsistency and you affect the experience, which inevitably devalues the product. This is especially true for enterprise products such as Airbnb that span differing technology stacks, devices, demographics, and so on. It is almost impossible to reduce the potential of design entropy without first directly addressing the company's workflows.

- *Version control goes out the window*: Both the design and development teams use a variety of tools that don't always place nice with each other. The upshot is the right assets may not be used at the right time and for the right purpose. Toss digital tools such as Adobe XD and Figma into the mix, and version control becomes an even bigger issue. If naming conventions aren't rigorously applied, there will be a huge issue with developers especially if design tokens are an integral element of the design system.

- *Inefficient processes yield repetitive or wasted effort*:
  A lack of a common toolkit for both development
  and design increases the very real risk of "one-off"
  solutions, which can be a huge drain on the team's
  efficiency. For example, without a design system,
  designers may be creating common elements and
  screens from scratch. Then those assets are handed
  over to the development team, and they will need to
  write the code for these "new" solutions.

We called them "common factors" because they are all connected
to each other. This is why it is so important to streamline the workflows
between the development and design teams. Don't streamline and the
pain of unscalable design and development is real, thus the need for that
single source of truth.

Where Do You Start?

There is a common misconception that you start with the fundamentals
like colors, typography, components, design patterns, and so on.
According to Dan Mall of SuperFriendly, that might just be a really bad
idea. "Design systems should be a collection of processes," writes Dan in
an article entitled "The Folly of Design System Foundations'" (`https://
superfriendly.com/design-systems/articles/folly-of-design-
system-foundations/`). "The best ones," he continues, "focus more on
what you can do and give you the tools to do it."

This is where it gets interesting because if you are an enterprise
organization with lots of sites and apps, then you approach it one way. If
you are new to the topic, then you likely will start another way.

For large or mature organizations, you are almost there. The first thing to do is to audit your current sites and apps looking for common patterns. Such things as type and color have most likely already been set, so why bother. For you, according to Dan Mall, a design system is a system for creating interfaces that integrate with other organizational systems.

If you are new to the game, don't waste time picking out just the right shade of blue or just the right typeface or worrying about the stroke thickness, size, and stroke color used with a card. Of course, you are going to need a color palette and typeface, but you need to build something, not waste time fretting about inconsequential details.

For those of you planning to put a design system into place, here are some suggested steps to get started:

- Create a foundation for a design system process.

- Document inconsistencies in the interface.

- Get organizational buy-in into the design system process.

- Build a small design system team.

- Organize design system sprints.

- Run the first seven to ten sprints.

- Organize retrospectives.

These steps are deliberately vague because no two organizations or teams will have the same approach. What we can say is this is a deliberative process and will take time to put together and deploy across the organization or the team. Getting deep into each step of the process is well beyond the scope of this book. As such the rest of this chapter will deal with design systems and your involvement in a very general manner.

Taking Stock of What You Have

To begin the process of scaling your design operations with design systems, you need to know the current state of your design and development ecosystem.

The best way to start is by building an inventory of all the different patterns, colors, text styles, and assets used in the product. The inventory is going to expose inconsistencies ranging from content to code and provide you with a good starting point. A good place to start the process is creating a pattern library.

The Pattern Inventory

We use design patterns in a number of ways. They offer feedback, tell the user how much time is left, give users the opportunity to select items, and so on. Design patterns can delight users, make tasks intuitive, and even give the user a sense of control. In many respects, the success of a project can hinge upon how these patterns are used and how they interconnect to support the UX Mission. From an enterprise point of view, there could be hundreds of these patterns, and we are pretty sure a lot of them are either out of date, rarely used, or even duplicates of each other. This explains why undertaking a pattern inventory and building a pattern library from the resulting pattern inventory is important.

The pattern inventory (Figure 5-1), often referred to as the component inventory, will yield a pattern or component library because... without a systematic approach, building digital products without this library is a recipe for chaos. You also need to be clear that the resulting pattern library is not the design system. It is a tool to be used by both the design and development teams for documenting and sharing the design patterns because multidisciplinary libraries both are able to adapt to change and have a very long shelf life. Build the library for either designers or developers, and the obvious friction will occur.

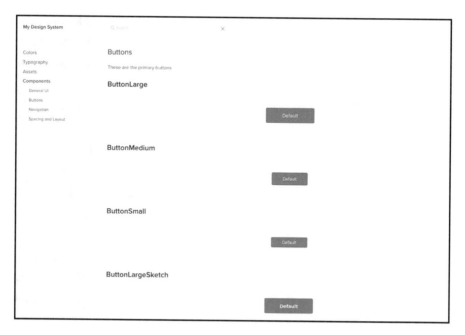

Figure 5-1. *A pattern library contains common components and design patterns*

A great place to start taking stock of what you have is to take screenshots of design patterns or go through your design projects to collect them. If you are using prototyping software such as Figma or Adobe XD, the screenshots or existing patterns can easily be added to a shared library available to the team. In this way, you have an inventory of the patterns and their variations. These can be used as the basis of the documentation necessary to aid your work.

As you collect existing patterns, it would be a great idea to check the front-end code and make sure the rest of the development team is aware of the architectural approach and accessibility accommodations used throughout the code base.

Try to identify if the front-end architecture is modular and if you can use it to categorize patterns in the inventory. It is quite common for front-end developers to employ a modular architecture that can be used within the design system to organize these patterns. If it exists, then use that architecture to categorize your collection. For example, if the lowest level includes such elements as buttons and switches, you might want to name a category "element switch" and include any links or tokens associated with that particular element. Do this and you can quickly identify any inconsistencies that may exist.

If a modular architecture is not in place, then it is critical that you categorize all of the inventory's patterns. Don't get hung up on architectural details. Simply look for common categories for the elements (buttons, cards, form fields, etc.), which will make it easier for the team and stakeholders to see where inconsistencies exist.

From a developer's point of view, a react.js library of components can be created and saved in Storybook. Storybook (storybook.js.org) is an open source tool for building component libraries, which can then be integrated into such prototyping tools as UXPin. One great feature of Storybook is it lets you build small atomic components, which helps you document your components for reuse and to visually test them.

The Color Inventory

If there is one source of chaos, color has to be it. Start to inventory the colors, and the odds are almost 100% there will be redundancies. We know of one inventory where there were 116 color variables with 62 shades of gray. To bring order to the disorder, start by combing through all of the code files and listing all of the color variables. That also includes any CSS files as well. Once you have that list, note the number of places where a particular color appears.

Once the list is complete, organize it by a common denominator in the color library. That includes all of the shades, hues, tones, and tints of say... the greens (Figure 5-2). Look at the list again, and you will be able to not only sum up the colors and their variables but also the odd varieties of a particular color such as just how many different shades of green there really are.

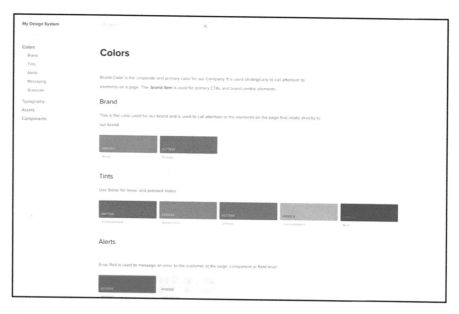

Figure 5-2. *A color library contains all of the colors and variations of those colors*

The Typography Inventory

If your project is complex, typography can quickly become unmanageable. Not imposing a typographic scale across the project results in a convoluted architecture and defeats the purpose of the UX Mission for the users. Also keep in mind that without a typographic scale, the odds are pretty good it is going to be rather expensive to maintain due to code fragmentation.

To start the inventory, consider opening the project's UI in a browser console and checking all of the text styles. Note any inconsistencies and resolve them by creating a typographic scale (Figure 5-3) that orders the typographical hierarchy (e.g., H1 down to small text). There also may be instances where tokens may be involved. If this is the case, try to match them with the styles in the inventory.

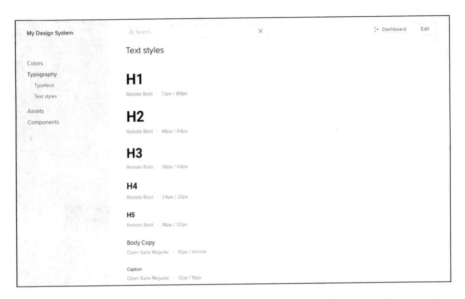

Figure 5-3. *When building the type library, include both the typeface and the type styles*

The Asset Inventory

It doesn't matter if this a one-off or an enterprise-level endeavor. There are going to be assets used throughout the project. These assets could be images used for personas, corporate logos and their variations, icons used in buttons and menus, animations, video, and even audio files. If this is a one-off project, then any assets used should be added to the asset library (Figure 5-4). If you are involved in an enterprise-level review, then inventory all icons used, look for duplicates, and remove them. When it comes to corporate logos, make sure you are using the current version of the logo and its variations. Images should be in the proper format such as .jpg or .png—and be sure that their scaling factor is clearly noted. Icons should be in the .svg format, and any size and color variations of those icons should be included.

Once all of that is in place, this would also be a good time to group them as shown in Figure 5-4. This not only makes the designer's life easier, but by grouping the assets and their variations, logic is applied to what could easily become nothing more than "a place to stick stuff."

Figure 5-4. *Once the asset inventory has been whittled down, assets can then be added to an asset library*

Design Tokens

From a developer's point of view, design tokens are indeed a single source of truth.

Design tokens are basically names used to express design decisions in a language to communicate design decisions between developers and designers. If we look at an app, it can be broken down into four distinct composition areas. An app is made up of its features. Those features are composed of interfaces. These interfaces are composed of components— and components are composed of design tokens (Figure 5-5).

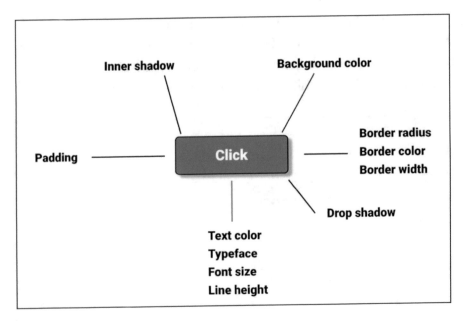

Figure 5-5. *Components are composed of design tokens*

Design tokens were originally developed by Salesforce as a way to enforce design consistency across all of their platforms. Their concept caught on because, through the use of tokens, design decisions are able to be stored in a platform-agnostic manner. These would be such fundamental decisions as colors, typography, spacing, and so on... that can be stored so that design tools can access them or transform them into something a developer can use. In fact, the W3C Design Tokens Community Group (https://github.com/design-tokens) is currently working on standardizing tokens in such a way as to make it easier for such prototyping tools as Figma and Adobe XD to incorporate them independent of the tool they were built in.

Design tokens move away from the generic naming of elements to a semantic naming convention. For example, instead of referring to colors for what they are, they are referred to by how they are used. For example, let's assume your base branding color is blue with a value of #2680EB. And it is used in a button component. That component will actually be a collection of design tokens (Figure 5-5), which describe how each property of the elements of the component looks when it is used. In this case, that base color may be darkened when rolled over or lightened when clicked.

That color could be expressed using JSON as

```
{
"name": "app-base-blue",
"value": "#2680BE",
"type": "color"
}
```

This is where the beauty of tokens comes into play. That example really doesn't reflect a background color other than to lock it in. Design systems offer options. In this case, colors can scale from dark to very light. Instead of naming the color... variables can be used instead:

```
$color-main-90 = #0E2D54;
$color-main-20 = #80C7F9;
$color-main-10 = #2680EF;
```

Even though the various options are available, that's all they are: options. They don't state where they can be used or applied to such contexts as the use of a light version on rollover. You can take the guesswork out of this Figure 5-6 by simply providing that context:

```
$background-color-dark = $color-main-90;
$background-color-light = $color-main-20;
$background-color-base = $color-main-10;
```

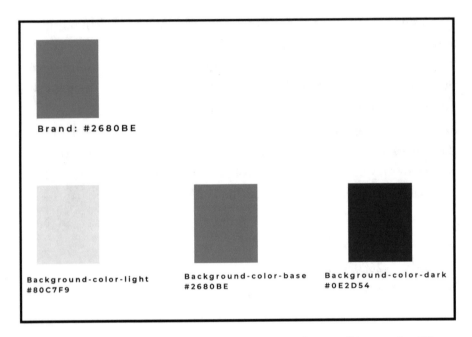

Figure 5-6. *Color swatches with context can be used in a color library*

Whichever approach is used—such as JSON, Sass, or YAML—to create these tokens, the document is usually located on some repo that doesn't help the designers. Though there are a number of ways of getting it to the designers, a popular tool that has the ability to do just that is Style Dictionary from Amazon Web Services (`https://amzn.github.io/style-dictionary`). What this free GitHub repo does is give you the ability to create and edit your styles and with a single command... export all of the rules to where they are needed—iOS, Android, CSS, JavaScript, HTML, style documentation, and so on (Figure 5-7).

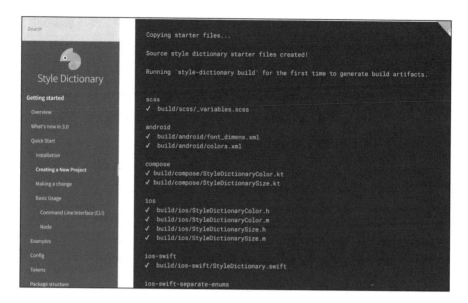

Figure 5-7. *Style Dictionary lets you create and edit styles and then export them*

Do this and the tokens are in one location and available to any product designer or developer who has adopted the system. The advantage here is that the token collection is available in easy-to-use, predictable formats. Hundreds of tokens now become readable decisions woven into a single project or an enterprise's collection of products. Change one token, say a darker background color for a button, and that value is propagated to every project or product tied to that design system.

Naming Tokens

We can't stress enough the importance of establishing a naming convention that provides the context so necessary for a token. In fact, basic names such as base-blue... simply won't work. Names must be descriptive enough to incorporate both classification and use—which infers enough levels are required in order for the tokens to be located in groups. For example:

- *Base*: These are the "fundamental" tokens that combine category, concept, and property—such as the blue used in a hover state.

- *Modifier*: These levels refer to one or more variants, states, scales—and even dark mode or light mode.

- *Object*: These levels refer to a component such as a button, an element within a component such as an icon inside the button, or even a component group such as forms.

- *Namespace*: These levels identify the design system such as myDS, a theme such as Dark Mode, or even a domain such as retail.

For example, the token $myds-button-color-hover-normal-10 could map to #0E2D54 because it combines four of those levels... $myds refers to the namespace, which, in this case, is the design system. The identifier button is the object, and color is the category. Normal-10 would be the base category.

Another way of approaching token naming is to take a look at Adobe's token naming approach. In the documentation outlining their Spectrum design system (https://spectrum.adobe.com/), tokens fall into three groups (Figure 5-8):

- *Global*: These are, in many respects, the base group. In this group, you will find the color palette, animation, typography, and dimension values are listed as global tokens such as #2680EF being targeted as blue-400.

- *Alias*: These are close to being in the modifier group. They relate to a specific context or abstraction. Their example is `cta-back-ground-color` that pulls in that global color.

- *Component-specific*: These fall into the object group and are a representation of every value associated with that component. They often pull in the values from the alias token but are named in such a way that engineering has no doubt about how specific the tokens are when the project moves into development. Their example is quite succinct: `button-cta-background-color`, which will change the color property to the blue in the alias category.

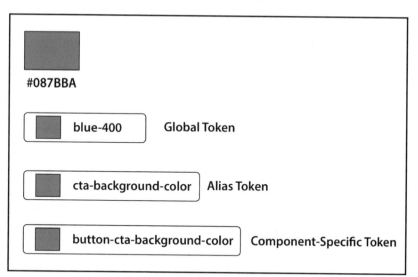

Figure 5-8. *The Adobe Spectrum token groups*

Conclusion

In this chapter, we have revealed why a Design System is, indeed, "the single source of truth." A comprehensive design system will not only significantly reduce development time but also reduce design time. By being available to both designers and developers, iteration time is also reduced because a change of a color's hue will ripple through the entire system and project, creating a consistent visual branding.

You also discovered creating a design system is a methodical process, which will most likely consist of forming a design system team composed of both designers and developers who will conduct a number of sprints involving reflection and iteration to achieve the final elements of the design system. This works well for enterprises, but if this is a one-off, then just jump in and start with the basics and build from there.

The first step in that process is to create an inventory of patterns, typography, and colors with the express aim of removing redundancies and reducing complexity.

Though the term "design system" may infer developers play a secondary role, we pointed out there are tools such as Storybook that allow you to write the JavaScript for component libraries and have them subsequently integrate with a prototyping tool such as UXPin.

The chapter wrapped up with a discussion of one area where you can play a major role—the implementation of design tokens. These documents could be written in such languages as CSS, JSON, and YAML. We then pointed you to Amazon's Style Dictionary, which lets you export that document to the common coding languages and even documentation, which can be shared among the team.

The final section dealt with the age-old question, "How do you name these things?" This is a complex subject because no two organizations or teams have common names. Instead, we suggested that tokens be broken into specific groups, whose, as the tokens get more complex, changed values will be inherited from the parent.

CHAPTER 6

The UX Design Process

Being a somewhat new field, the user experience community hasn't done a great job of standardizing its job titles yet. A quick scan of user experience job postings will unearth a grab bag of titles: Ux designer, Ui designer, user researcher, customer experience researcher, interaction designer, user experience architect, usability engineer, graphic designer, visual designer, Web designer, copywriter, tech writer, content strategist, design strategist—and infinite permutations of all of the above.

—Leah Buley
Rosenfield Media
"The User Experience Team of One"

When asked to define the term "UX," one of the authors turns the question around and asks, "What do you want it to mean?" This answer is not the author being facetious or dismissive. Instead, it recognizes there is no commonly accepted definition of the term. When you come to grips with

© Tom Green and Joseph Labrecque 2023
T. Green and J. Labrecque, *A Guide to UX Design and Development*, Design Thinking,
https://doi.org/10.1007/978-1-4842-9576-2_6

understanding what UX is all about, you can get a clearer picture of the scope of a UX design project and the job of the UX designer. To start, let's answer a few common questions:

- What is UX?

- What is UX design?

- What does a UX designer do?

First, What Is UX?

UX is short for "user experience." When we say "user experience," we refer to how people experience a product, either positively or negatively, and form opinions around that product based on their experience.

For some reason, UX is regarded as a relatively new arrival to the digital design scene. Nothing could be further from the truth. Go to a local museum and look at a pottery vessel. Depending on its shape, size, and so on, you instantly know it is a cup, a pot, or a bowl. We also intuitively understand how people interact with that item. You drink from a cup. You cook in a pot and eat from a bowl.

Knowing what the item is and how to use it works when presented with a relatively simple item. In our digital world, things aren't simple. They are complicated. Your car's dashboard has become complex as the standard gauges and warnings are not where you expected to see them. Go to the appliance store; the typical refrigerator is now sporting a screen connected to the Internet and is somehow "smart." Who needs to see a bank teller when the bank is on your smartphone? All we need to do is invest some time to understand it. Then, again, what happens when something we intuitively understand does not function as we understand it? Should when we interact with it?

This is where the terms *affordances* and *signifiers* come into play. For example, we interact with a door when we want to enter a store. The design of the door—including the color, material, and physical appearance—tells us (signifies) this is a door, and doors afford opening and closing. In even more succinct terms, a door affords (is for) entry and therefore affords opening and closing. Then we try to open it. If you push it inward, the door opens, and the experience is positive. However, if we push it only to discover it won't open because it needs to be pulled, that is a negative experience, especially if nothing tells the user to pull the door open. A sign on the door saying it must be pulled is the signifier (Figure 6-1).

Figure 6-1. *A bus door that tells you what it does is good UX*

Like that door, in the digital design world, UX refers to everything affecting a user's interaction with a digital product. We all know what a button on an interface is supposed to do, but without the text, we don't know what it does. When people use a product, they usually evaluate their experiences according to the following criteria:

- *Value*: Does this product give me value? Not knowing what a button does because there is no signifier makes the experience valueless.

- *Function*: Does this product work? A button that does nothing, an experience we have all had at some point, tells us the button doesn't function as expected.

- *Usability*: Is it usable? A button on a smartphone that is out of reach of your thumb or is so small it won't work is a bad experience.

- *General impression*: Is it pleasant to use? For example, if you expect to push the door open and discover you need to pull it open, the first impression is not nice, especially if your arms are full of packages.

Don Norman, a co-founder of the Nielsen Norman Group, coined the term "user experience" in the 1990s. According to Norman, "User experience encompasses all aspects of the end-user's interaction with the company, its services, and its products." When apps and websites became the norm, UX became important because companies had made serious financial investments in their digital products. As any marketing professional will tell you, the whole point of marketing is to create and keep a customer. If their app was complicated for their customers to use, they would abandon or even delete it or leave their shopping cart where it was and go elsewhere. Above all else, the purpose of UX is to make the experience as friction-free as possible for the user.

Other important aspects of UX include the following:

- User experience is people. People can be both rational and emotional, and whether you care to admit it, users will react to a product both rationally—"This button doesn't work"—and emotionally, "The button sucks."

- User experience requires a provision of context. People using the parking app will be either sitting in their car or standing on the street to use it.

- The experience usually involves a learning curve. The goal is to keep that curve as short as possible. When first using the parking app, it will most likely take someone a few minutes to figure out what to do. That time will decrease to a minute or less as they become familiar with it.

UX doesn't mean one thing. One of the most significant pitfalls for anyone new to UX is understanding UX as separate from other related fields (like web development, technical communication, etc.).

UX is an interdisciplinary philosophy. It is a way of looking at the world that involves making decisions beyond data with humans firmly in mind.

With those points in mind, you start to understand why UX has grown in prominence and the job of UX designer is not close to what many think it encompasses.

What Is UX Design?

UX is almost always followed by the word "design." By the very nature of the term, people who work in this field are commonly known as "UX designers." It is a very vague term that can be interpreted in a variety of ways. As we ask at the start of this chapter: "What do you want it to mean?"

UX designers don't design experiences. What UX designers do is to direct the project in such a way that users create a good impression of the product.

UX design, like UX, is a process. In fact, creating products that both are usable and contain what Google calls "delightful details" is a complicated process.

Peter Morville's UX honeycomb (Figure 6-2) from his article around user experience design presents what he calls "facets of user experience":

- *Usable*: Ease of use is paramount.

- *Useful*: Are the products and systems that support them innovative and practical?

- *Desirable*: Everything on the screen counts. This includes images, brand, and so on that are designed to result in a positive emotional response.

- *Findable*: Everything on the screen must be able to be found, and this includes navigation.

- *Accessible*: Accessibility is not a nice-to-have. We don't control whether the person using the product is able or disabled.

- *Credible*: With all of the misinformation out there, a brand must retain its credibility, so users actually believe what they are seeing or being told.

- *Valuable*: The product or service must deliver value to the stakeholders.

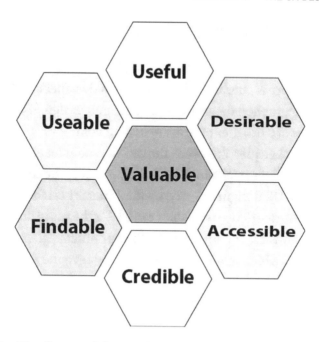

Figure 6-2. *The facets of the UX honeycomb from Peter Morville*

With that in mind, the UX designer's role is not simply designing the screens or pages of a digital product. It is far more encompassing than that. They need to design digital experiences in such a way that they are understandable. At the same time, they need to be both the user's and the client's advocate.

If the UX designer has done their job, users will instinctively understand how to use the product, thereby protecting the client's investment. This can only happen when a carefully choreographed dance between data and design occurs.

Dancing Between Data and Design

UX design can't occur in a vacuum. You can't make it up as you go along. Do that, and failure is guaranteed. Thus, the UX designer's role is a carefully choreographed dance between data and design. UX designers are usually part of a broader product team and commonly find themselves bridging the gap between the users, the development team, the design team, and the business stakeholders. For example, in the case of the parking app, the UX designer must consider what is best for the user and that individual's experience with the product. At the same time, the UX designer is responsible for ensuring the final product aligns with the app's corporate vision, which might include increased revenue and customers.

Having established there is no commonly accepted job description for a UX designer, there are some general functions that a UX designer performs, including

- Conducting user research

- Creating user personas

- Determining the information architecture of a digital product

- Designing user flows and wireframes

- Creating prototypes

- Conducting user testing

Just keep in mind these are generalizations. For example, in a corporate project, the UX designer may focus more on the first three than anything else. However, if it is a startup, those tasks and more will be involved, including working closely with the development team.

Setting the Scene with Research

Ask any UX designer where a project starts; the answer is always research. Many UX design positions focus heavily on research where the UX designer conducts or manages the research. When running the research phase of a project, many of the tasks would include

- Interviewing users and stakeholders to get a sense of user needs and the business requirements.

- Performing a competitive analysis to analyze the strengths and weaknesses of a competitor's product.

- Conducting online surveys to gain a deeper understanding of features that may or may not be included in the project.

- Conducting focus groups. The UX designer may convene focus groups to get a deeper understanding of how people will use the product. If budget permits, the UX designer may even retain the services of a company to conduct the focus groups.

When the collected data is analyzed, it is used as a basis for decision-making during all phases of the production process. For example, the data collected and analyzed would be incorporated into such tasks as creating user personas, determining the information architecture, designing user flows and wireframes, creating prototypes, and even conducting user testing at various stages during the workflow.

As a developer, being exposed to, if not involved in, the research phase is invaluable. You gain an insight into who will use the product and what they expect to see. Collaboration with the UX design team becomes invaluable as the information architecture is created. You start to gain insights into the front-end and back-end tasks that may need to be undertaken. In the case of the parking app, you begin to get an idea of the

115

scope of the work ahead of your team. For example, you know you must create a payment management system. There will have to be an account creation process and some way of managing the time purchased, among other things. You aren't going to develop them, but you can start planning for their implementation. Being involved in the research phase is much more efficient than being handed the prototype and told, "Wire it up."

UX Design Is a Team Sport

You could infer from the previous sections the UX designer is a jack-of -all -trades. Nothing could be further from the truth. The UX designer is an integral part of a team, which is why we regard UX design as a team sport.

When a typical project involves a website and a mobile version targeted at iOS and Android smartphones and tablets, you can't reasonably expect one person to do it all. In the current environment, mobile and web are synonymous. Even web-only projects need to be optimized in such a way they provide the user with a similar experience on their smartphone as they would have using their computer's desktop browser. As we said earlier, things got really complex really fast. Specialists inevitably replaced generalists, and here, briefly, are some of the members of a team and what they do:

- *The client*: You may find it odd to see the client. However, clients need to be included because the UX designer is the client's advocate as well as the user's advocate. Therefore, the client will be regularly briefed on the project's progress and involved in the approval process.

- *UX designer*: The individual or team responsible for the complete user experience from research, design, and testing.

- *User researcher*: The individual or team responsible for gathering data through interviews and observation to inform design decisions.

- *UX writer*: The UX writer is responsible for creating user-friendly content for the product and ensuring the integrity of the project's messaging.

- *Visual designer*: This is commonly a team-based role responsible for creating the visuals such as images, icons, and screen design that align with the product's design strategy.

- *Motion designer*: This team member prepares the animation and visual such as micro-interactions or how screen elements move from one location to another. Motion design also includes the creation of animated GIFs or LottieFiles animations.

- *Interaction designer*: The individual or team responsible for creating the user interface interactions. This might strike you as a bit redundant. Not quite. Interaction design aims to create interactions that are intuitive.

- *Prototyper*: Sometimes referred to as a UI designer, this individual is responsible for designing and testing prototypes that validate design decisions.

- *Usability specialist*: The individual or team responsible for conducting regular usability tests to ensure the product meets user needs.

The UX design process has also gotten complex for developers as well. Here, briefly, are some of the traditional development roles when it comes to UX design projects:

- *Front-end developer*: Responsible for coding the user interface for the product, including HTML, CSS, and JavaScript and even additional, specialized languages and frameworks for the chosen platform(s).

- *Back-end developer*: Responsible for coding the server-side logic for the product, including databases, APIs, server-side scripting, and the development of server-based systems that support the front end by managing data flow and retrieval.

- *Mobile developer*: Responsible for coding the mobile application for the product, including using native languages such as Swift, Objective-C, Kotlin, or Java.

- *Quality assurance engineer*: Responsible for testing the product to ensure it meets the requirements and functions as expected.

- *Technical writer*: Responsible for writing technical documentation for the product, including user manuals and tutorials.

None of these roles acts in isolation. As a team sport, collaboration is the key to success. For example, a motion designer may create a multiplatform LottieFiles animation using a system of authoring tools, conversion services, and playbacks. Rather than hand the animation over to the developer with the expectation the developer will make it work, the developer may, instead, request the JSON file that makes up the actual LottieFiles animation or even the embed code if it is being placed in an HTML page. Of course, this only happens if the motion designer is talking to the front-end developer.

Another example would be the UX designer discovered, during the research phase for the parking application, the parking attendants use a portable scanner to scan the vehicle's license plate to check if the car has paid for parking. The back-end developer should know this requirement well before any design and brainstorming get underway. The back-end developer will then work with the UX designer and the client to ensure the app information gets passed to the client's system and from there to the scanner.

One final example would be the UI designer handing the prototype off to the usability specialist who then subjects the prototype to various user tests. The results show some issues with the interface, colors, text, and icons. At this point, the UX designer, the UI designer, the writer, and the visual designer will review the results with the usability specialist and develop a plan to solve those issues.

This is why we sometimes refer to the UX design process as "messy."

Artifacts and Deliverables

No UX design project proceeds from concept to upload without regular reviews, approvals, continuous testing, and "tweaking." It is also safe to say that no UX design project moves through the process without creating and circulating artifacts and deliverables. Though we provided a general explanation of these in Chapter 2, let's get a little deeper into the subject.

Before listing some of these items, you may wonder about the difference between an artifact and a deliverable.

Artifacts are such design items as a motion graphic, the prototype of a login sequence, or a component residing in a GitHub repository. Artifacts are generally circulated to selected team members for critique, testing, or review.

Deliverables, in general terms, are documents, prototypes, and other material circulated to the team, including client stakeholders, for the purposes of information, review, and approvals.

There is no standard regarding which deliverables and artifacts will be created for a UX design project because no two organizations and projects are identical. Common deliverables for a UX design project could include user journey maps, wireframes, user interface prototypes, user flows, personas, user research reports, usability testing reports, design guidelines, and style guides. Deliverables usually fall into one of the following four categories:

- Project documentation

- User research

- Design

- Testing

Project Documentation

- *Business requirements document (BRD)*: This document makes the business case. It carefully explains what is needed, why it is needed, and who needs it.

- *Technical design documentation (TDD)*: This documentation defines what technology and implementations have been selected to address the needs as identified in the BRD. It will lay out the platform(s) that has (have) been selected, configurations, templates, and versions of software and hardware.

- *Product and functional requirements documentation (PRD, FRD)*: These are prepared by the engineering team and lay out specific technical details, infrastructure specs, configurations, and security solutions.

The purpose of UX documentation is to provide a basis for rational decision-making and should be made available to all team members. This would include designers, developers, QA specialists, stakeholders, and management—all of whom may (or may not) use a particular document to make business or design decisions regarding their work.

User Research Deliverables

- *Personas*: Personas are fictional characters, based upon user research, who represent a class of users who would use the product in a similar manner (Figure 6-3). Personas give both the designers and the developers an opportunity to keep these people in mind while they work on the project.

Figure 6-3. *A typical persona. Personas are snapshots of mythical users created from user research*

- *Journey maps*: These are visualizations of how a user could interact with a product from the user's point of view.

- *User flow diagrams*: These diagrams, circulated to the developers and the designers, represent how a user would navigate through a project. These diagrams make it easier to identify which steps need to be redesigned or improved.

- *Task flow diagrams*: These diagrams (Figure 6-4) are more granular than user flows. They focus on how a user completes a simple task, such as registering a new user. As a developer, these diagrams aid you in developing the coding requirements to accommodate the task.

Task: User wants to log into the application

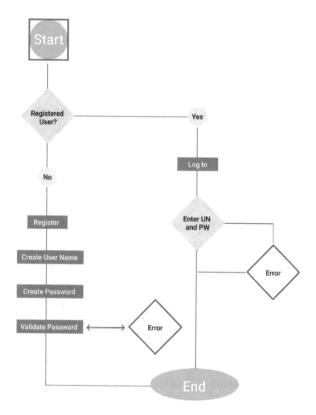

Figure 6-4. *A typical login task flow*

- *Use cases*: This describes how a user will perform tasks in an app or website. These are always from the user's perspective, and each use case is presented as a sequence of steps starting with the user's goal and ending when that goal is achieved.

- *Experience maps*: These are diagrams that explore the various steps users take as they engage with the product. They are invaluable aids for the designers in understanding the user's motivations and needs at each journey step.

123

Design Deliverables

- *Sketches*: No UX design project starts on a computer. They always start with a piece of paper and a pencil or pen. It is a quick way of visualizing a new home page design because, as we constantly say: "You can't describe it. You have to show it." Sketches are a way to validate concepts and design approaches with the involvement of all stakeholders, including developers and even users.

- *Wireframes*: These are where the sketches start to come to life. They are a visual guide to the proposed page structure and hierarchy of crucial elements of the screen (Figure 6-5). Their focus, to be blunt, is to show where stuff goes, not what the stuff is. Again, these can be produced on paper or digitally; once approved, they are circulated to the stakeholders.

  If developers are expected to code an HTML prototype straight from wireframes, then it's important to give them as much information as possible. If you prefer wireframing on paper, we recommend the "sketching in layers" technique, which uses increasingly darker shades of gray since it provides more structure and detail than standard freehand sketching.

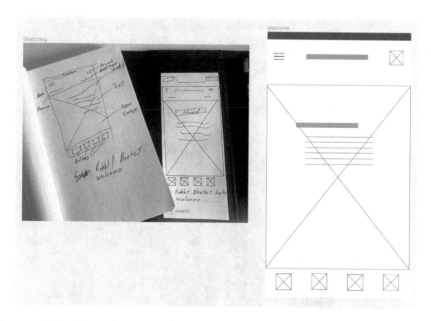

Figure 6-5. *Everything, including wireframes, starts on paper*

- *Prototypes*: These documents come in three flavors:
  low fidelity, medium fidelity, and high fidelity. Low
  fidelity could be a paper prototype of each screen of
  the wireframes sent out for user testing or a collection
  of wireframes taped to a wall or even drawn on it.
  The low-fidelity wireframes could be assembled in
  prototyping software and circulated. Medium-fidelity
  prototypes contain all of the imaging, text, and line
  art assembled in prototyping software such as Figma
  or imaging applications such as Sketch or Photoshop.
  Finally, high-fidelity prototypes are essentially the
  fully interactive version of the project from a prototype
  created in prototyping software that gets handed off
  to the development team along with all of the assets
  contained in the prototype.

125

One major development feature of the prototyping tools is they give the developer an opportunity to inspect the code (Figure 6-6). Some even go as far as to let you view the code used for iOS and Android development. Whether you use it or not is up to you.

Figure 6-6. *Inspecting code in Figma. Figma lets you choose CSS, iOS, or Android views*

- *Design system documentation*: Your design system or style guide outlines the product's design patterns, fonts, colors, components, hierarchy, spacing, and other visual design standards. The design system will also include guidelines and correct usage to maintain a single source of truth across the organization. If the design system library contains tokens, getting those to the design team can be a huge issue. In many instances, the technical writer will create the documentation, update the design system, and store it in Amazon Web Services' Style Dictionary or some other service or location, which we discussed in the previous chapter.

Testing Deliverables

- *User testing report*: This document summarizes the issues users raise when they use the product. User tests are commonly done at each phase of the product and confirm or invalidate any user assumptions made at each step. We will get a bit deeper into this in the next section.

- *Usability testing report*: This report, circulated to the team and stakeholders, summarizes any usability issues clearly and concisely that helps the team become aware of a problem and work to resolve it. There will always be usability issues, but these reports tend to summarize their severity, which helps the design and development teams determine where to start.

User Testing Is an Iterative Process

It is all too easy for the project team to get caught up in the tangle of documentation and so on from the start to the finish of a project. By focusing on the project, they have an intimate knowledge of how the product works—they most likely won't have an intimate understanding of how humans work. What users may say and what they do are polar opposites, and the only way to verify is to test early and test often. The results of these tests will either validate or blow up your design decisions.

We are well aware every company and each project are different. If they were all the same, a standardized usability test would tell you all you need to know every time. This is "magical thinking" because it doesn't exist. Instead, define your hypothesis, determine which method will test it, and get ready to get really uncomfortable.

Testing identifies user issues with a product, and user testing at regular intervals allows the team to refine the product or solve the problem much earlier than sending it out for user testing at the end. The upshot is user testing will result in iterations of the product. In many cases, each iteration is sent out for user testing to ensure the issues identified are resolved.

User testing is a rigorous process. You can't design a login sequence and then wander around the office asking what people think and leave it at that. On the other hand, most prototyping software allows for sharing; the comments received are invaluable and invalid. The reason is the commenters are "too close" to the product, so they know how it works and what it does.

To find out what people really think, you need a clear goal. If you don't know what information you want to obtain before you conduct your test, you risk launching a test that inevitably fails to yield actionable insights.

The other aspect of why we regard user testing as an iterative process is because instead of one, all-encompassing test, it is easier to run a series of smaller ones that have a single objective. Do this, and the team is more likely to get focused results that guide the team to an iteration that solves the issues or supports a decision or change made before the test.

Remember: you don't need to uncover every issue or problem in an exhaustive study. While it's tempting to try to cover as many challenges as possible, running a series of smaller studies with one specific objective for each is much easier and more productive. In addition, you're more likely to get focused feedback that guides you toward a solution or supports a decision or change.

Regarding developers, one may think they are nothing more than observers. Not quite. Developers should be aware of all testing results that may not involve them. What they may glean from those results will be a piece of solid information that could impact both the front-end and back-end development teams.

Let's assume you want to test logging into the parking app. The designer has designed the screen, the front-end developer has wired up how to pass that information to the server for verification, and the back-end team has the process to verify the information.

The objective here would be: Can the user successfully log in?

Two critical items popped out of the test. First, one user had an issue with the two-step verification. A modal overlay told the user a text would be sent to the user's mobile device, which arrived 1 minute later. Another found the modal information too hard to read.

Obviously, things need to be sped up on the back end or front end. Also, the writer may have to simplify the text, or the designer needs to revisit the design of the modal. Finally, it only makes sense to test it again to ensure users are happy.

Conclusion

In this chapter, you have discovered why UX has become so important and misunderstood. We explained this using the example of a door that should open when pushed. If there is nothing there telling the user to pull the door open, that is regarded as a bad experience. As we pointed out, UX is a way of looking at the world that involves making decisions that go beyond data to decisions that fall in love with the user, not the technology.

You also discovered the role of a UX designer is to design the experience, not the screens. In many respects the UX designer guides the team. We walked through the various roles of both the design and development teams and emphasized that the UX design process is a collaborative team sport.

Finally, you have gotten a pretty comprehensive look at the developer's role in the UX design process. As you have seen, your participation, suggestions, and input are just as invaluable as those whose roles are not development oriented. You play an important role in all aspects of the project from the research phase to user testing. You also saw there are a number of "deliverables" that are commonly produced and circulated to the team and the stakeholders.

As we pointed out, UX is a team sport. Designers need an awareness of how the interfaces work, and this awareness will ripple through the entire UX Process. Similarly, you, the developer, have to become familiar with the design language, design systems, and style guides that visually communicate their intent. To achieve this, open collaboration and clear communication are the best way to move through the UX Process because there are a lot more people than a UX designer involved.

CHAPTER 7

The UI Design Process

Although designers may not fully understand the development cycle, it's important they treat developers as members of the same product team—otherwise your design will fall victim to unnecessary compromises and nasty surprises.

—UXPin
"The Designer's Guide to Collaborating with Developers"

In the first chapter, we made it clear the UX Mission focuses on falling in love with the user. UI design is the process that shows that "love." In fact, UI design is a process that supports the UX Mission laid out in Chapter 1. The issue, in today's UX environment, is there is no such thing as a UI designer because there is no common understanding of exactly what "UI design" means. The Internet is bombarded with individuals showing off a screen or collection of screens they have created and claiming they improved the UI of a particular brand or created an example of a UI to demonstrate their skills. That is not UI design.

UI design involves the creation of all the visual elements that make up the project's user interface... from the first screen to the last screen. Depending on the scope and complexity of the project, the number of

© Tom Green and Joseph Labrecque 2023
T. Green and J. Labrecque, *A Guide to UX Design and Development*, Design Thinking,
https://doi.org/10.1007/978-1-4842-9576-2_7

screens could range from a half dozen to a couple hundred. Those screens are how a user interfaces with the project, and user opinions regarding the utility of the project are formed regardless as to they're being on the splash screen or choosing a shirt color. Though a design system imposes design consistency, there is a lot more to UI design than the design system.

A UI needs to

- *Be consistent in design*: Design consistency is a lot more than the logo in the upper left-hand corner of a screen. We have no control over where a user will land or go, and, to the user, each screen needs to be what we call "a familiar place."

- *Support the business and branding objectives*: A design system does just that, but the design of a UI is composed of the bits and pieces of that design system. Each screen needs to be a "unified whole." A great example would be the Starbucks app (Figure 7-1). Each time the authors wander into their local Starbucks shop, the Android and iPhone devices are firmly clutched in the patrons' hands, and the app makes it dead simple to purchase a menu item because there is a big green "Scan in store" button within handy reach of a thumb.

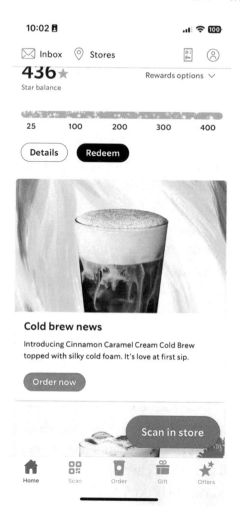

Figure 7-1. *The Starbucks app not only supports the branding objective, but the order button is within reach of your thumb*

- *Be intuitive*: The whole mission of UX is to fall in love with the user. When it comes to UI design, that means the user should never encounter a screen and wonder, "What do I do here?" or "What does this error message mean?" That big green "Scan in store" button right on the Starbucks home screen is intuitive. It tells you exactly what to do. It's placement and size are reachable using your thumb, and that green color is part of the Starbucks brand.

- *Have a logical flow with no barriers to understanding*: Apps and websites fail not because they are poorly designed but because they are simply too hard to use. A great example of this is something one of the authors constantly encounters. When purchasing an item, the shipping information requires one to select the state or province. Being Canadian he looks for his province in the drop-down list, and not one Canadian province is listed—or he selects the province, and an error appears prompting him to select a state.

- *Be engaging*: Google has a term when it comes to UI design that it calls "delightful details." A great example of this would be the lowly Floating Action Button from its Material Design specification. There are all sorts of things you can do with this button, which Google designed to grab the user's attention. When rolled over it gets a bit larger and changes color. When clicked or tapped, it shrinks a bit and maybe even changes color. Everything it does is subtle, and creating that subtlety is the job of the UI designer.

As you may have surmised, UI design is a lot more than the placement of pretty pictures, text, and animations on a screen. The UI design team has the overall responsibility of creating the visual elements that make up a UI, and that includes the visual hierarchy and placement and size of everything from the layout, colors chosen, the choice of font, the design of buttons, menus, and other interactive elements that make life easier for the user. It doesn't stop there. They must also consider the size, resolution, and other technical aspects of what devices will be used to view the project. The requirements for Android, iOS, and the Web are fundamentally different from each other. Not only that, the requirements for specific Android and iOS devices vary between the device manufacturers and need to be considered. This is just plain common sense, but there is another important reason for this attention to detail. It will make the developer's life easier.

Tip   When considering UI design for iOS, Android, and other established systems... keep in mind that there are often robust design and development guidelines that take a lot of the guesswork out of how to appropriately design UI elements for each particular system. One example of this is the guidelines for Google's Material Design—which we will touch upon in detail later in this chapter.

UI Design Is a Team Sport

It is common to see individuals promoting themselves as UI designers. This is not a bad thing because depending on budget and project scope there may not be the resources for a full team but there will be resources for a few generalists. Having said that, the days of the generalist are slowly coming to an end. As one of the authors is fond of saying, "This stuff got too complex too fast." We are moving toward "specialization" and away from generalization. As such, UI design is evolving into what we call a "team sport" where a team of specialists bring their very specific skills to bear on a project as needed.

Though there is no common team makeup, a few of the specialists that may or may not be involved in the UI design process would include

- *UX designer*: As you discovered in the previous chapter, the UX designer is responsible for the overall look, feel, and flow of the project and ensuring the business objective are met. The documentation produced will guide every aspect of the UI design workflow, and that includes user flow diagrams, wireframes, and even user testing the design at various points in the workflow.

- *UI designer*: This role is responsible for developing the visual elements of the user interface. This could include creating what are called mid-fidelity prototypes that are static designs for each screen created in such applications as Photoshop or Bohemian Coding's Sketch. These screens follow and expand upon the wireframes. They could also be responsible for creating the high-fidelity prototypes that are created in specialized prototyping software such as Figma, Adobe XD, or UXPin. Conversely, there could be a specialist whose sole task is to create the prototypes in conjunction with the development team.

- *Interaction designer*: As you may have guessed, they design all interactions from how buttons function to how a user navigates between the various areas of the final project. This individual might even be the one responsible for pulling together the interactive prototypes. It goes a little further than that as well. An interaction designer will conduct user tests to ensure certain interactions meet user needs. For example, a test may discover users are more comfortable with a side menu that slides in from the left rather than appearing as a drop-down. On top of that, the interaction designer will work closely with the development team to ensure the "intent" of a particular interaction is achievable.

- *Motion designer*: The motion designer is responsible for creating the animations and transitions that remain faithful to the project's intent without getting in the way of the user. Animated onboarding sequences are a good example of what this role encompasses. The animation must both support the business and design objectives while also providing the "delightful details." The motion designer walks a fine line between the animation being nothing more than entertainment and achieving business objectives. This individual typically uses specialized software to create these animations and will work closely with the development team to ensure they receive the code and assets that drive the animations and motion.

The Design Language

Though those are just a few of the roles, there is a common thread running through the UI design process. All the team members must be on the same page and speak the same language, which, in this case, is the design language.

A design language is not what we call "techie talk." Do you really understand "We were creating vectors but, realizing we couldn't use an .ai file, we were faced with choosing between the .svg and .pdf formats that used the sRGB color space"? That's jargon, and you can just imagine the look on the faces of the stakeholders when presented with this during a design review.

A design language is what describes the overall visual and interactive design style that is consistently used throughout the project. Through the use of consistent colors, typography, layout, icons, animations, line art, and so on... the user will intuitively know what to do, where they are, and what each element on the screen is supposed to do.

This is the all-important role of the design system. It provides each team member, including the front-end and back-end development teams, with clear, documented guidelines for the use and properties of anything that will appear on a screen.

Google's Material Design site, material.io, is a great example of a design language. Not only are the design specifications laid out, but they also provide examples of their usage. In Figure 7-2 Google is showing what you can and can't do with a Floating Action Button. This sort of directive is invaluable.

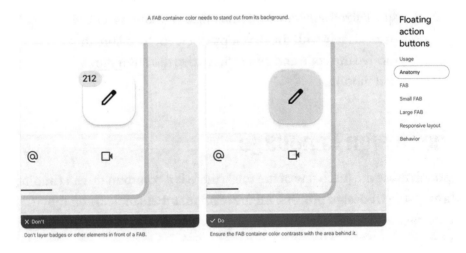

Figure 7-2. *Google clearly explains what you can and can't do with a Floating Action Button*

Being shown examples of what you can and cannot do provides concise usage directives for the UI design team. Yet, there is much more to simple usage when it comes to creating the design language. It is a living document made available to both the design and development teams. In Figure 7-3 NASA's Jet Propulsion Laboratory has created a design system using Storybook from Amazon Web Services. In this example, the use of an element of type `BaseImagePlaceholder` is discussed—including when and how it is to be used. Through this resource, the developer can grab the HTML code when it is time to use this element as a placeholder. An important aspect of this example is it lays out exactly why this element should not be considered accessible and it also presents the properties associated with this particular element.

Figure 7-3. *NASA uses Storybook to present the design language*

Getting Started with a Design Pattern Library

Once the UX documentation has been finalized, the flow diagrams are agreed to, and a full set of wireframes have been completed and approved, the development and design teams not only have a clear idea of the scope of the project but a very rudimentary idea of how the screens will look and function. What they don't have is any idea of how interactive elements such as buttons or drop-down selectors will look and function. This is the point where the design language starts to come to life.

This process commonly starts with the construction of a design pattern library. As you work through the wireframes, you will notice certain elements, such as buttons, appear everywhere. From the perspective of a user, they know exactly what a button is and does because they are everywhere. They have used them. They understand them. Users are recognizing a pattern. They recognize a button and, instinctively, match it with what they have previously experienced with a "button."

Let's face it; creating and coding multiple instances of the same button on a few dozen screens simply makes no sense and, to be honest, is a colossal waste of time. This is where design patterns come to the rescue. Design patterns are common interface elements that, when turned into components and incorporated into the design system, provide that all-important element of design and function consistency. In addition, users are quite familiar with what these common UI elements do, which is why changing the look of a hamburger menu icon because you want it to look "cool" is not such a great idea.

Common design patterns include such elements as

- *Hamburger menu*: Why is it so commonly found in websites and apps? It provides extra space for the presentation of a side menu or drop-down menu, for example.

- *Cards*: Cards have become ubiquitous spreading out from the first iteration of Google's Material Design specification for Android to iOS and the Web. Cards, as shown in Figure 7-4, are condensed information sources—usually containing an image, text, and a button—that deal with a single bit of information. The great advantage to these elements is they all contain a common design and function just as well on the desktop as they do in the confined space of a smartphone.

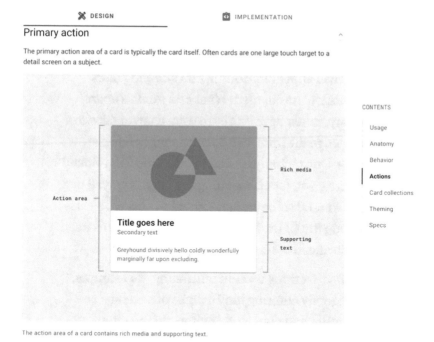

Figure 7-4. *Cards are common design patterns*

- *Drawers*: Typically associated with hamburger menus, the slide-out drawer presents the user with navigation options. Drawers are extremely popular on devices, thanks to the limited space. Again, users intuitively understand how to use them. Each strip could contain both text and an icon. If this is the case, the text needs to be both explicit and concise, and the icon should be one commonly used elsewhere so as not to confuse the user.

- *Modals*: The purpose of a modal is to draw the user's attention to something they might have missed. One of the authors lives in Canada, and, every now and then, when ordering something from a US-based company, a modal will appear informing him shipping rates to Canada will be charged. What sets modals apart from simple messages is they require a tap or click to acknowledge the information or to simply skip the message. One technique used to make modals noticed is they are given focus, meaning the page is grayed out or blurred until something is tapped or clicked. This is something the UI design and development teams need to decide ahead of time.

- *Input hints*: Nothing is more infuriating, for example, than diligently entering the 16 digits of a credit card number and constantly being told the input is incorrect. Two things can happen here. The user abandons the transaction, or the user keeps trying only to discover adding a space between the number sections results in success. In either case, making life easier for the user was ignored. Adding a series of dots or grayed-out numbers into the input field—the hint—makes this a more pleasant and achievable task. Again, it will be incumbent upon the UI designer and the developer to work out how this data will be incorporated into the component.

Prior to the components being designed and developed, it won't hurt to ask if there will be a dark mode variation of each component. With the components in place, they should also be tested or shared with the team two or three times throughout the design and development cycle. This will isolate potential design and/or development issues, which are easier to address now than at the end of the project. Once all the approvals and finishing touches are obtained and completed, they can be moved into the design system and made available to the UI design team.

Creating Content

A full component library with the requisite color and typographic standards makes life easier for all involved because, in very simplistic terms, they are "create once, use many times" elements that can quickly be added to a screen. Even then, a screen is composed of other content such as images, line art, video, audio, and animation. These items also require the developer and the UI designer to be aware of their unique requirements. Let's look at a few of them.

Imaging

Photographs support the message and, it goes without saying, they need to be free of copyright and, if people are in the photos, the UX designer needs to obtain the proper releases. Once that has been settled, there is a major issue that will need to be resolved even before they are added to a screen. It is "scaling factor." This is strictly related to how many pixels are jammed into one linear inch of a particular device's screen. For iOS devices the factors range from 1x to 3x. Android is what we refer to as the wild west with factors ranging from .75x to over 4x as the Android device manufacturers compete more on resolution than anything else. It makes sense, therefore, to determine the target devices before production starts. Don't use them, and as shown in the following, the experience is not a good one.

In Figure 7-5 the device used is an iPhone 12. The image on the left has the proper scaling factor of @3x, whereas the one on the right has a scaling factor of @1x. Both images have the same physical dimensions (375 × 375). The one on the right is displayed across 375 pixels. The one on the left has the proper scaling factor (@3x) applied to enable it to display across 1,125 device pixels. As a developer it is incumbent upon you to request the images handed to you have the correct scaling factor applied.

Figure 7-5. *Incorrect scaling factors make for a really bad experience*

Tip There is a fundamental difference between scaling an image to fit and applying a scaling factor. Scaling an image does nothing more than put the same number of pixels in a larger or smaller space. A scaling factor is a mathematical calculation that increases the number of pixels to accommodate the higher resolution of the device chosen.

There are two common imaging formats—JPG and PNG. JPG is what is known as a "lossy" format. What this means is when the image is converted, it is compressed to reduce the file size. It is during this compression that pixels containing colors that are close to others are "lost," thereby reducing the file size. The UI designer will normally apply a compression value to these images.

PNG or Portable Network Graphics was developed as a replacement for the JPG format. What distinguishes these images from their JPG cousins is that PNG files can contain transparency, which can increase the file size, and they use a form of "lossless" compression—which makes the compressed files much larger than a comparable JPG since the extra information is not discarded outright but is rather compressed to decrease the file size. Of course, removing the data altogether results in a much smaller file size when dealing with a JPG. As the developer, the file size increase in a PNG can directly impact download time. Again, a policy behind the use of each format should be established between the UI design and development teams prior to production.

We also can't overlook the GIF and animated GIF formats. Though they may or may not make it into the final product, they have several uses throughout the UI design process:

- *Creating micro-interactions*: The animation or motion crew may use them to demonstrate these small, subtle interactions with a website or app. For example, a GIF could animate a simple hover effect to demonstrate the designer's intention.

- *Demonstrate product features*: A GIF or animated GIF is a quick way of showing the team how a specific feature works.

- *Provide feedback*: Rather than a LottieFiles animation or CSS-driven motion, animated GIFs can be used as loading animations as content loads or to simply confirm to the user their action has been registered.

As mentioned earlier, a GIF likely will not make it into the final product. This is simply because while GIFs do have their benefits in prototyping and design... it remains an ancient and restricted format. Formats such as LottieFiles, small videos, or animated SVG will look and perform much better within our more modern technology ecosystem.

Line Art

Line art is traditionally vector-based, and the file format is Scalable Vector Graphics or SVG. This content is commonly created in a drawing application such as Adobe Illustrator or Bohemian Coding's Sketch. The most common use for line art is for icons. The beauty of the SVG format is it is code driven as shown in Figure 7-6. Should you need to "tweak" the code, you can, but this should be done with the approval of the UI design team.

Figure 7-6. *Developers can access the .svg code if necessary*

Animation

Animations, when done properly, can seriously improve the experience. This could be something like an onboarding sequence where LottieFiles or CSS animations control the movement. In the case of LottieFiles, the motion designer may work out the motion and ease in an application such as After Effects. Once the motion or animation has received all the necessary approvals—including approval from the development team—the file can then be exported out as a LottieFiles animation from After Effects and, if requested, the resulting JSON file can be handed over to the development team.

Tip   It isn't just animations. The property changes for the components in the design system can also be driven by CSS animations or LottieFiles.

Video and Audio

When it comes to working with video and audio files, two things are important: format and delivery.

The common format for video is the MP4 container format using the H.264 or H.265 video codec and AAC audio codec. The purpose of both is to compress both tracks to ensure smooth playback. This is where delivery becomes critical.

Video delivered to a web page through a desktop browser is not an issue. Delivering that same file through a wireless connection to a smartphone can be problematic. The key is to set the data rate to one that is optimized for wireless delivery, not to mention keeping the file size low. Ignore both and the video will start and stop as the browser or system cache empties and refills. Therefore, it is important to test video and audio files prior to release.

Tip   To keep audio files manageable when delivered to a smartphone or tablet, consider changing the file to mono instead of stereo and reduce the data rate to between 60 and 80 kbps. The effect will be a significant file size reduction.

Pulling It All Together with Prototyping Software

With all of the assets created, the UI design team will start creating the prototype containing all of the interactions, animations, and motion. Though all prototyping software does essentially the same thing, we are going to focus on two applications: Figma and UXPin.

Before we get going, there are a few things you need to know:

- Prototypes can be low, medium, or high fidelity. Low fidelity would be something like the wireframes in the form of a click-through. Medium fidelity would have all of the assets in place, but functionality is limited. High-fidelity prototypes are fully interactive working simulations of the final product and, in their final form, are ready for handoff to the development team.

- Prototypes are disposable. Once they are handed off to development, they will essentially be ripped apart.

- Prototypes can also be used to demonstrate intent and ask for feedback. For example, the UI or interaction designer could create a simple button that, when clicked, rotates and three more buttons move out from behind it. As the developer, you could look at the code behind it to get an idea of what needs to be done. At the same time, the UI design team could provide feedback, and the project may go through several iterations to get the interaction and motion just right.

- Prototypes are commonly sent out for user testing and are then revised based on the results of the test.

149

With this overview of prototypes, let's now turn our attention to two applications where they are created: Figma and UXPin. We have chosen these particular pieces of software because Figma is one of the most popular UI design applications with tons of features and plugins that appeal more to UI designers than developers. UXPin has features that will appeal more to UX developers. Just keep in mind they are just tools and the choice of which to use is up to you.

One very appealing feature of each one is they are browser-based, making the sharing and collaboration of the UI design process extremely easy. Both have a desktop version of the application if the browser isn't appealing to the individual using the application. In both cases, the desktop application is basically a container for what is available through the Web—meaning changes made on the desktop versions are instantly available to those using the browser. We'll start with Figma.

Figma

As a browser-based tool, Figma is accessible to the whole team. There is a desktop version, but it connects to the web-based version, meaning functionality is the same regardless of what you choose to use. In many respects this accounts for Figma's popularity as a prototyping tool among UI designers.

As a developer there are several features that will make your life easier. They include

- *Code introspection*: Select an element and over in the Properties select the Inspect tab. You are then presented with three code view choices: CSS, iOS (Figure 7-7), and Android. As a developer you are not expected to use this code, but you can copy and paste the code into your code editor as boilerplate and change it if you so choose.

Figure 7-7. *The Figma UI lets developers introspect the code based on platform*

- *Red lines*: Select an element in the frame or artboard, and red lines appear giving you precise spacing and measurement data.

- *Properties panel*: Select a text block, and the full typographic specs are available. Select an element, and the full specs including constraints are presented. This is all handy information to have available to you.

- *Variants for component management*: You can create variants of a master component right in the Figma design space (Figure 7-8). The interesting aspect of this feature is the variants are all contained in the master and can also be documented.

- *FigJam*: This interactive white board has become extremely popular with teams for brainstorming ideas and concepts.

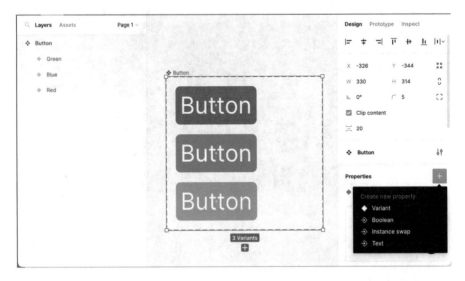

Figure 7-8. *Variants of master components can be created in the master component*

- *Flow and animations*: Select an interactive component, and in the Prototype area, you can see the trigger, the action, and the transition. You also can discover the properties for the eases used and their duration.

- *Export*: When it comes to handing off the assets to the development team, there are a couple of choices. This is something to be determined between the UI design and development teams. Assets can be exported individually or all at once. Just be aware that text will be exported either as a PNG or JPG. If this doesn't work, then PDF or SVG may be your best choices.

UXPin

Where Figma is the tool of choice among UI designers, UXPin (Figure 7-9) places equal emphasis on development as well. Containing all the features a UI designer will need to create a prototype including designing the prototype in Figma and then importing it into UXPin, this application also has a robust documentation feature and direct access to component libraries such as Material Design and additional systems and frameworks. Like Figma, UXPin is a browser-based application, which means developers can also access the designs, introspect the code, and so on.

Figure 7-9. *The UXPin interface*

Where UXPin really shines for developers is using its Merge feature. What it does is to hand both the UI design and UX development teams the ability to add Storybook components (Figure 7-10) created in react. js directly to your prototypes. As well… you can choose to import React components from a NPM registry or directly from a GIT repository.

Once those components are in place in UXPin, changes to them can be made either in UXPin or elsewhere, and those changes will ripple through the UXPin document and component library from Storybook or elsewhere. As a developer you can change the args in the react.js document, which will also ripple through the UXPin project, or those args will appear in the UXPin Properties panel and changes to those properties will be propagated to the react.js component.

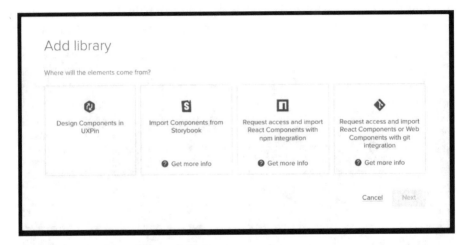

Figure 7-10. *UXPin's Merge accesses the component libraries and adds them to the project's Library panel*

Conclusion

In this chapter you have discovered the term "UI design" is vague and generally misunderstood. As we said right at the start of this chapter: "UI design involves the creation of all the visual elements that make up the project's user interface… from the first screen to the last screen. Depending on the scope and complexity of the project, the number of screens could range from a half dozen to a couple hundred."

We also made it clear the role of the UI designer is just one part of a broader team of specialists ranging from an interaction designer to a motion designer who bring their skill set to bear upon the project at various points in the design process.

The process usually starts with identifying the common design patterns to be used throughout the project and developing a common design language, which is a comprehensive document that not only contains the designs of the design patterns and components but also clearly lays out how each item is to be used in the project. This should also include the developer's input, and, in many cases, this document can be contained in a GitHub repo or Storybook library where the elements can be added to the project and where the developer can access the code that makes them come alive.

From there, we briefly reviewed some of the content types that make up the elements on a page ranging from images to audio and video files. We also presented aspects of each content type that you, the developer, should be aware of.

Once the content is created, it is inevitably added to a prototype. Though prototypes are a great way of demonstrating intent, you, the developer, will rip it apart as the project moves into the development phase. This is why we point out that prototypes are "disposable."

You also discovered there are three types of prototypes based on fidelity. The low-fidelity or "LoFi" prototype is usually composed of the wireframes where the emphasis is on where to content will be rather than the content itself. These can be digital or paper prototypes and can be subjected to user testing.

The medium-fidelity or "MidFi" protype is a static design that is commonly created in such applications as Photoshop or Sketch though they can also be assembled and lightly coded in prototyping software. Their purpose is to not only demonstrate, visually, the UI designer's intent but to also gather feedback around the screens. In fact, the designs may undergo several iterations based upon this feedback. Another use for

MidFi prototypes is to demonstrate both the design and functionality of the important components in the library and to gather feedback. Again, there could be several iterations of these components before they are finally approved and added to Storybook or a GitHub repo before they, too, are approved and made available to the UI design team.

The high-fidelity or "HiFi" prototype is where the entire project is assembled and contains all the functionality of the final design. These prototypes are commonly subjected to user testing and team feedback and, based upon the user testing and team feedback, can also undergo several iterations before final approval and handoff to the development team.

We finished the chapter with a broad overview of two prototyping applications—Figma and UXPin—not as an endorsement of these products but to explain prototyping software can lean more toward UI design or more toward developers. The choice of prototyping software is made well before the project moves into the UI design phase, and what prototyping software to use is up to the UX design and UI design teams.

CHAPTER 8

Development

Supposing is good, but finding out is better.

—Mark Twain

In the preceding chapters, we examined many considerations when it comes to the user experience and user interface design. The next step in the UX Process is to prepare for the development phase of our product. We do this by not only planning next steps but also grounding our plans to be looking backward at all the data that has been gathered through previous phases of the UX Process.

When it comes to development processes, one of the most important things to consider is how you will work with designers for a successful implementation of the assets, designs, prototypes, and specifications handed over to you. As a developer, you should always be open to various opportunities that may present themselves within the process. These opportunities can include the discovery of new data that you must then incorporate into your existing plans, flexibility with the tools used between different groups working within the product space, and doing whatever is necessary to get the right design within the finished product.

Within this chapter, we'll be examining the importance of keeping an eye on previous work—alongside current developments—to discover additional opportunities through keeping the data in mind. We'll also explore the importance in establishing a working relationship between

T. Green and J. Labrecque, *A Guide to UX Design and Development*, Design Thinking, https://doi.org/10.1007/978-1-4842-9576-2_8

designers and developers at the crucial phase of the process. We must emphasize how important grounding the current work is, through the work that has already been done, which leads up to this phase of the overall process. We will have a look at some tools and workflows that can be used across designer and developer teams for greater productivity, organization, and collaboration. We'll finally examine the importance of testing and knowing when to pivot based on the data gathered from your tests.

While the development phase is critically important for the UX Process... the truth is that it should never be worked upon in a vacuum. Reliance upon new ideas, data, and methods—even during heavy development—can make a world of difference in the resulting product and how users will eventually react to the experience.

Opportunities for Discovery in Development

As we enter the beginning of the development phase of the UX Process, we should keep in mind everything that has led up to this point and keep our perspective open to adjusting our approach when new information comes along. A hugely beneficial set of data may still arrive from prototype feedback being sifted through and organized... and, perhaps, even potential user testing that may be going on with beta versions of the product.

As diagrammed in Figure 8-1, research and testing should both feed the design and development processes. In addition, research can better inform and improve testing, while testing can provide additional avenues of research. This is a complex and messy part of the UX Process with so much information going in so many directions. A good rule of thumb to go by, as new sets of data are discovered, is to keep everything as organized as possible. Organizing your existing data—as well as any new data that comes to light—in a meaningful and applicable way is beneficial to all stakeholders, including designers and developers.

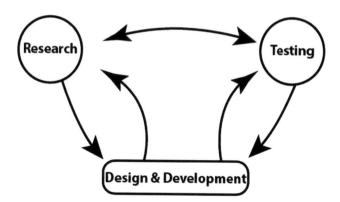

Figure 8-1. *Even in the development phase of a project, you will still want to keep informed with any new data that is made available. Remember, research should be continuous!*

There are a number of ways through which your team might consider making use of discoveries derived from new sets of data. This includes the following considerations as you enter the development phase of the UX Process:

- *Organized data analysis*: When your data is well-organized, certain patterns cannot help but emerge as you dig in and examine the resulting information—whether it is derived from direct feedback, user testing, or even hidden analytics in an existing product. You can monitor these patterns across time to get insights into how your users are working with the product.

- *Data-driven design*: Once the data has been organized and patterns have been identified, it is much easier to leverage what you have learned from examining this information to help steer the direction of both design and development trajectories. Based upon user reactions to the product or even a prototype of the product, everyone can make better decisions around any changes in direction or improvements to the overall design. Of course, these design changes will also spill over to influence the choices you will make as a developer.

- *Collaborative transparency*: This is more of an internal mechanism to gathering feedback on your work but is still important in the overall umbrella of the UX Process. It involves collaboration between all project stakeholders and gathering feedback from them early in the process and continually as design and development moves ahead. While many stakeholders are not traditional users, they do care deeply about the product—and anyone with such high stakes should be consulted often for feedback and impressions. This information should be shared with the entire team to be most effective.

Note   Concerning Mark Twain's quote from the beginning of this chapter, "Supposing is good, but finding out is better," consider how it applies to the process of letting the data continually inform the design and development phases of your product. How might your suppositions negatively impact choices you make in development? Isn't it truly better to be certain or, at least, more certain about your direction and choices?

No matter how you gather and structure the data, such methods of discovery during this phase of the UX Process are still incredibly important. Even if no major adjustments arise from the data, all stakeholders have an easy-to-access, organized view of everything that's been gathered via disparate processes all in one place. Not only can important decisions be more easily made in such a situation… but there is transparency involved as well—which can help everyone feel more as though they truly are on the same team working toward the same goals.

Interactions Between Designers and Developers

As we have emphasized throughout the preceding chapters, cooperation between different teams is a critically important aspect to consider when working through the UX Process. As we've said before in this book, one of the most beneficial cooperative relationships in this process is that which can exist between designers and developers. For a long while, these two groups were often considered separate from—and often in opposition to—one another. These days, organizations and teams are coming around to realize that both groups are important members of the entire organization and that their collaborative work on a project can be massively beneficial to the entire process.

Instead of the design team tossing some prototypes and assorted assets and specifications over the wall to the development team and then waiting for a return answer, it is much more productive to form real relationships across both teams early on, which can be taken advantage of during both the design and development phases of any project. Working together, in tandem, across a table is so much more effective and supportive. For instance, while producing assets for the developers to implement within a product, the designers should have a chat with the developers to talk about expectations and restrictions (Figure 8-2).

Working in silos

Working in tandem

Figure 8-2. *Designers and developers should be working together for their own good and for the good of the user*

As you saw in Chapter 2, certain target platforms will have unique requirements for deliverables depending upon the intent of use. If the designer does not recognize these specifics, the assets provided to the developers can be wildly incorrect in format or particulars. The most effective way to get around any such problems is to maintain a good working relationship with one another and to maintain regular discussions around the work being done.

Tip   Encourage the design team, early on, to become familiar with developer guidelines for the chosen target platforms and to work with one another to develop common terms of understanding between designers and developers. Not only will this assist in ensuring that designers have a basic idea of certain expectations and platform restrictions… but it will also facilitate discussion and goodwill across your teams while guiding communication and results.

One last thing to consider when dealing with your relationship with members of the design team is the co-creation of interactions. Communication between teams is necessary for a good outcome, but how might that be taken a step further? Both designers and developers being open to true collaboration during the design phase can open many more channels of interaction. Developers can give technical direction and make suggestions during the design phase and learn first-hand the reasoning for certain interaction design decisions. Designers can gain insights into platform specifics and the more technical requirements of deliverable assets as they build product prototypes in order to more closely align with developer expectations. While not every organization is equipped for close collaboration, it is always something worth investigating.

Looking Back to Get Ahead

At this phase of the UX Process, it is important to keep sight of where you are considering all the work that has occurred so far—especially with an eye toward those phases that have come before. Decisions made in previous phases of the overall process—and the reasons for those decisions—are all essential information in framing the current phase of development. Use what you know about the previous work to form your own approach to the tasks that lay directly before you, and it will be difficult to disappoint others.

Tip   You, as the developer, should take responsibility for acquiring this information in case your involvement in the process to this point has been lacking due to any number of possible factors. These factors could be intentional or unintentional, and it is always best to assume no ill will. If you've been kept in the dark on certain items, request a one-on-one with other stakeholders to get up to speed with the project history. If you have had the fortune of continual involvement, all the better for everyone!

One of the best tools at your disposal when looking back to what has been prepared prior to the current development phase is the design system. We've examined design systems before—but how can this tool assist in the development phase of the process? As a developer, being provided with assets and documentation can be a great help... but getting access to a true design system can really help clarify any items that come into question during the handoff.

For instance, you may receive a description of the confirmation button to process payment for our parking app example. This description could include the colors used, typeface properties, positioning information, and so on (Figure 8-3).

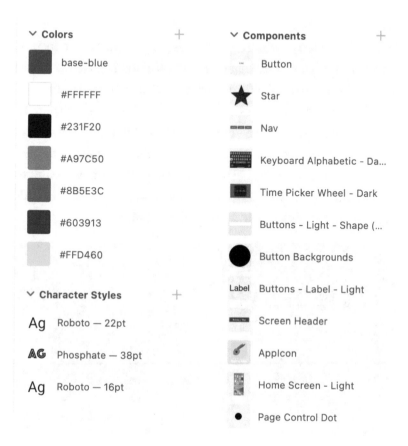

Figure 8-3. *A design system, if made available to you, is an essential tool in achieving parity with the overall product vision*

The design system will give you, as the developer, a lot to start with... but if you had access to the actual design system—the single *source of truth* for the project design elements—you might imagine how much more confident you would be in ensuring that what you produce matches what has been designed beforehand. Another essential tool at your disposal is the actual design prototype. Getting access to the prototype—and not only assets and information derived from the prototype—will allow you to view design elements in context with all other elements. Of equal importance to this is the fact that the prototype provides design agency for you as the developer. It is your chance for exploration and discovery... to look back at what has been produced by the design team not as a consumer of information but as an active, engaged, and thinking individual or team.

Using the tools and specialized views that are included in most all design and prototyping software, you will be able to select specific elements across unique screen layouts in order to gather information that can aid in development. You are not only able to explore simple elements like images and text across each screen but can also explore how individual components and their variants or states are established along with all intricate details of their design (Figure 8-4).

Figure 8-4. *The specific asset properties from a prototype can inform and guide the development process*

The fact that this information originates directly from approved prototypes will once more provide you with a greater sense of confidence as you proceed with your work.

Recall as well that these tools present even more opportunities for discovery as development proceeds and the actual product takes form. If you, as the developer, arrive at certain questions about what decisions have been made in the past or how specific functionality should play out... you can—and should—have ongoing conversations with the design team. Learning more details about the conclusions they arrived at in the design system and prototype during the UI design and UX design phases is a great way to ensure that the final result is ideal for all stakeholders. At this point in the process, you should even make suggestions upon how the existing designs may be adjusted and refined to either improve the development process or the overall user experience.

Keeping in line with our theoretical parking app... consider that the development phase of the product design process should include some of the same measures as when parking a car (Figure 8-5). Taking the necessary precautions and staying aware of what lies ahead but also keeping an eye toward what is going on behind you will provide the safest driving experience.

Figure 8-5. *While parking a car, you must keep tabs on activities both in front of you and behind. You should take the same measures and precautions during the development phase*

The situational awareness required when driving and parking a vehicle is that you must continually look forward and backward to consider all possibilities—all in determination of what will work best for the user of the experience being produced. If the design team cares about the success of the product, they should be open to developer inquiries and feedback. Questions about the process and outcomes should be welcomed as any resulting changes may positively impact the product for all involved.

Organizational Tooling and Sharing Data

With a proper perspective obtained through determining your current place in the overall UX Process and surveying the work that has already been performed, it is time to consider some additional tooling and ways of sharing information with your colleagues. Truly, the best tools to choose in most situations are those that can be used by both designers and developers. Why? Because this allows for closer collaboration and an increase in the sharing of data. If everyone is invested in the toolset and finds value in usage outcomes, it will be much easier to ensure constant collaboration and dedication while working through any issues that arise.

As a developer, you are likely very familiar with Git repositories and related web-based services such as GitHub. While you can certainly use Git as a version-controlled code repository alone, GitHub is an interesting service in that they have built up a number of additional tools and workflows around this core product. Not only does that add value to their services, but it adds that value across teams so that everyone can contribute—not just developers.

A great example of this is GitHub Projects (Figure 8-6)—a flexible tool for planning and tracking work across the lifetime of a project. You can imagine that planning and tracking are useful across all areas and not just for the development team specifically even though GitHub is traditionally seen as a developer tool.

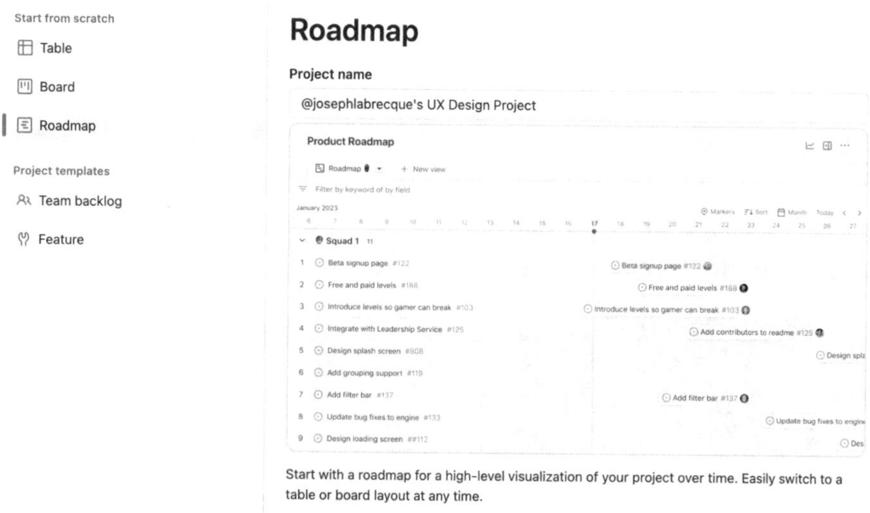

Start with a roadmap for a high-level visualization of your project over time. Easily switch to a table or board layout at any time.

Figure 8-6. *GitHub Projects supplies a great set of tools that can be accessed by all stakeholders—not just developers*

What's great about using something like GitHub Projects is that you can involve researchers, designers, managers, and other stakeholders early for a more tight-knit collaborative environment in the same location that you will be committing your code and tracking development issues.

Having all of this data accessible to all contributors... in a single location... is invaluable. It's likely that similar tools will be used by the development team—so why not open it up to additional functionality? This approach also makes for a great resource once your product has launched, and you can look back across the entire recorded history to perform either a project debrief... or to plan future updates.

Note   While we highlight GitHub Projects in this section, remember that this is just an example. There exist a growing number of collaborative tools in this space, and you should always choose what is best for you and your team.

Another great collaborative tool is the prototype itself. Most design and prototyping tools include a mode that can be used by the development team to extract useful information in the form of colors, positioning, size, motion, and other properties for various screens and nested UI elements. In Figma, for example, you have access to boilerplate code for various platforms, including CSS, Android, and iOS, from within the Inspect workspace with an element selected (Figure 8-7).

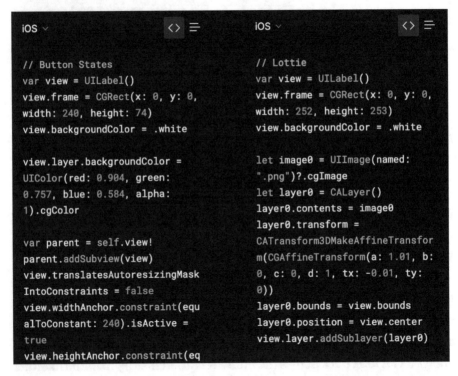

Figure 8-7. *Many prototyping tools will generate basic boilerplate code for design elements as a jump-start to implementation*

These can all be generated from the various asset types in use as UI elements in your project. By copying these boilerplate bits of code for import into the development environment, you are able to quickly transfer the design into a functional part of the experience on the platform of your choosing.

Normally, designers will share the prototypes they've created with the development team, allowing each developer to inspect and make use of whatever information they need to proceed with the work. At other times, the design team will collect this same boilerplate code into another document for sharing and distribution across the organization. No matter how it is shared, the important thing is that sharing occurs so that everyone is informed and has the proper amount of information to perform their work effectively while keeping in mind project goals.

Test Often and Pivot as Needed

When most developers think of testing, they probably jump straight into unit testing while programming the product code base since this is the aspect of testing you have the most direct control over. Oftentimes, any user testing is performed by another group within the organization—as we mentioned in Chapter 7 when talking about interaction designers—and then the results are relayed back to the design and development teams for adjustments. This is a good form of collaboration and ensures that information is shared to all stakeholders that can have an immediate impact on the user experience of the product. However, there are additional methods of testing that can occur between designers and developers that should not be overlooked.

Any testing should be performed based upon the scope of development but should also take into consideration exactly which phase of the overall UX Process you are currently involved in. Additionally, consider what other teams and individual stakeholders are currently working on to make an informed decision around what to test, how to go about testing, and whom to involve in these tests. When working in any sort of collaborative workflow, these routines can help you, as the developer, to more closely collaborate with designers working on the project—as well as speed up the iterative process. Any choices you make will also impact why and how testing is achieved—so keep that in mind as you make these decisions.

There are a few considerations around development, organization, collaboration, and testing to consider at this phase:

- *Setting goals*: This should be fairly simple to establish as so much work has already been completed for the project. From UX research to sketching and design and to full design systems and prototypes, there is a lot of existing material for you, as the developer, to build upon. If the project goals have not been defined at this point, that would be a very rare occurrence!

- *Choice of platform*: In alignment with project goals... you, as the developer, should already have a good idea as to what platforms will be targeted for this particular product. It could be a web-based project... or Apple iOS only... or target both iOS and Android. Depending upon the native platform being targeted, the technology stack will need to change as well—and this is something that the project's designers hopefully have had a handle on for a while now as designing for a specific platform is designing for user expectations... If you get this wrong, you *will* hear from your users!

Caution   If you've been in software development long enough, you might recall the Adobe AIR SDK being introduced to enable the creation of mobile apps for both iOS and Android using the same code base. When this technology first became available on iPhone (after existing on Android alone for a time), a lot of users were very critical—since there was no way to make use of the native iPhone UI controls and when Android apps were published to iPhone... which resulted in many AIR-based apps using their own custom UI, which was identical across Android and iPhone.

Familiarity means a lot to the user, and if things appear strange when using a product… they will uninstall and complain. While it is primarily the designer's job to ensure the UI matches platform guidelines, you can also ensure familiarity fidelity is in place.

- *Choice of framework*: With one platform (or multiple platforms) chosen, the development team will likely use whatever their common frameworks are for addressing each platform. Some consideration should also be given to the particular features of the product. The reason is certain frameworks are focused on specific types of experiences and are inclined toward the needs of such experiences rather than others. Always make an informed choice.

- *Choice of tooling*: As we saw earlier, the choice of tooling can greatly impact not only the development team but also the design team and anyone else who is involved in the project at this phase. At times, it may be prudent to make changes to the tools being used depending upon the platform and framework choices— but also the general needs of the project as identified by prior research and design. As we mentioned earlier, if tooling can be leveraged to assist multiple teams across the product lifecycle—especially across design and development teams—many things will be much smoother than if isolated tools are chosen.

- *Iteration and collaboration*: Provides a great opportunity for testing across teams and specific member expertise since you are working quickly through idea iterations and additionally collaborating with designers and other members of the larger organization. The intention of working quickly through these iterations has a lot going for it—but in order to be most effective, you should be mindful of organization and keeping track of the results of each test.

When testing at these various stages, no one should be deterred from changing direction and performing a complete directional pivot when necessary. If there is some problem identified with the product goals, the choice of framework, the tooling, or any other aspect of the project... it would be worth your time and effort to explore these considerations and even pause development or perform a drastic pivot when necessary. Going along with our previous car analogy... would you not pivot out the way to avoid colliding with an obstruction—like a trash bin—in the road (Figure 8-8)? Of course!

Figure 8-8. *Certain situations demand that you pivot at any expense*

In a lesser way, pivoting from your intended path when the need arises in the development process is also often necessary—though it can incur some short-term expense and setback. The development team may need to toss out blocks of code that took days to write simply because of such a change in direction. You may need to realign priorities and tasks within the team—causing significant disruption. Hopefully, once you've all reacclimated, you can look back with confidence knowing that any such changes have been beneficial to the project.

Conclusion

While this chapter was all about development, we didn't really address any code or programming practices. This might seem a little odd if you are more used to programming books. As you know, actual programming is just part of the job of a developer. The interpersonal communication between stakeholders and specifically your interaction with designers are an aspect of the developer's role that is often barely addressed.

With the present chapter behind us, what have we covered? First, we examined the importance of discovery within the development process and the ability to look for opportunities to learn more as development progresses. We then took a good look at different methods of interaction between designer and developer teams and the benefits to establishing a good working relationship toward the sharing of content and ideas. Midway through the chapter, we examined the usefulness of tools such as design systems and prototypes within the development phase and that keeping an eye to what has come before in the process is beneficial—and necessary—to have greater confidence in the direction of your work. We then had a brief look at some additional services to assist the already established collaboration between the designer and developer teams and again the importance of sharing both assets and data. Finally, we considered the ramifications of a hard pivot when coming across the inevitable crossroads in the development process. Should you continue in the same direction even though the data says a change is needed? Think carefully!

In the next chapter, we'll take a deeper dive into the subject of user testing as we continue to explore the UX Process.

CHAPTER 9

User Testing

It's important to remember that the UX design process is recursive, meaning that it almost never proceeds in a linear fashion.

—Guiseppe Getto
UXPin ebook
UX Design: The Definitive Beginner's Guide

Testing is humbling. You may have created what you think is a killer approach to a problem only to discover the User Testing results show it is difficult to use and understand. User tests should be conducted frequently and the timing and type of test is determined right at the start of each project.

Let's assume the parking app has a green Confirm Payment button at the bottom of the UI. Tap it, and your parking session is validated. Data from the gathered test results comes back, and one of the common issues is people keep assuming that button tells them their parking session has been validated. We are willing to bet you are thinking, "That's silly. They should know it has to be tapped to validate the parking session." Of course, they should. You have what we call a "knowledge bias." You know exactly how it works because you made sure it works. You know what it does. The users don't. If this is your reaction, then you have just discovered the value of testing. The user challenges your assumptions, and if it is a significant challenge, you have a couple of decisions to make: ignore it or deal with it.

T. Green and J. Labrecque, *A Guide to UX Design and Development*, Design Thinking, https://doi.org/10.1007/978-1-4842-9576-2_9

The question then becomes: If you choose to ignore it, are you prepared to absorb the cost of fixing it when the app is released? On the other hand, if you decide to deal with it, are you prepared to absorb the potential system and redesign costs to resolve the issue? As pointed out in the previous chapter, it is a lot cheaper to deal with it now.

Somebody will inevitably raise the Return on Investment (ROI) issue when testing is discussed during the planning process. In many respects, ROI is a nonissue because the implications of not testing include reduced employee efficiency, increased development costs, and even loss of customers. These are valid arguments, but the upside—significant cost savings or increased revenue—is a somewhat effective counter to the issue. The benefits of testing include reduced development costs, revenue increases, and happy customers.

Testing gives you a deep insight into how your users can use the product (Figure 9-1). When issues are uncovered, they can be resolved before they get baked into the code. It is commonly understood it costs ten times more to fix something that has been coded than to deal with it at the specification phase of the project. That may not be the case regarding your work because no two projects or companies are identical, which is fine. Even so, that button color change we wrote about earlier in this book is an excellent example of the implications a simple button color change can have on an entire code base.

Figure 9-1. *Testing challenges assumptions arising from the research and the design that meets those assumptions*

Why Testing Is Important

Throughout this book, we have consistently used the phrase "user testing." In fact, it is the title of this chapter. However, it is not quite correct because user testing is just half of the process. There are actually two types of tests: user testing and usability testing. They are different evaluation methods often used in designing and developing products. However, they have differing goals, processes, and outcomes. Though they may be different, they have one thing in common: they focus on the UX Mission.

The fundamental difference between the two approaches is user testing focuses on all users, while usability testing focuses on a specific segment of users. Another difference is user testing looks for ease of use, whereas usability testing examines whether people will actually use the app. Where they differ involves the validation of the various hypotheses from the research. User testing validates the hypothesis, whereas usability testing validates the design.

Let's look at each one.

User Testing

This method involves observing and interviewing real or potential product users to understand their needs, preferences, expectations, and behaviors. User testing is usually done in the early stages of design and development to inform the design decisions and validate the user requirements. In addition, user testing can help answer questions such as

- Who are the users?

- What are their goals and tasks? What are their pain points and frustrations?

- What are their motivations and values?

As you may have guessed, user tests are invaluable during the project's research and initial design phases. During the research phase, you get a real good look at the potential market, and these user tests validate or invalidate your design decisions.

Usability Testing

Usability testing is a method that evaluates how easy, efficient, and satisfying it is for users to interact with a product, service, or system. Usability testing is usually done in the later stages of design and development to measure the performance and satisfaction of the users. Usability testing can be done using the prototype. Putting the prototype in the hands of potential users can help answer questions such as

- Does the product meet the user's needs and expectations?

- How easy is it for users to learn and use the product? How quickly can users complete their tasks?

- How many errors do users make?

- How satisfied are users with their experience?

Usability testing can be done at various points in the process. For example, you could ask users to walk through a specific task such as setting up a parking session using the prototype, identifying and resolving the issues raised and doing yet another usability test to learn if the issues have been resolved.

Tip Don't forget usability testing also includes ensuring the accessibility features are also in place and tested.

It is also not uncommon to send bits and pieces of the UI out for usability testing at various stages throughout the design process.

For example, that Confirm Payment feature may have been dealt with by redesigning the button and adding an alert thanking them for their payment. As the developer, you need to ensure confirmation data is received when the button is tapped and the alert also appears and disappears over the set time. The designer may have designed two versions of the button and wants to know which one is more visible and meets the user's expectations. Even small changes may have significant implications. If the Confirm Payment screen is also shown in the onboarding sequence, then the motion designer must also make the change. These things are best caught now rather than when the app is released.

One of the things the authors constantly stress is: "Test Early. Test often."

Testing early and often is far more cost-effective and efficient to discover if the app or website meets the identified user needs, and you also get to watch the users stumble their way through the product. To this point, you have relied upon the research to design a product based on the identified potential users' needs. By watching them use the product, you gain a deep insight into what users do rather than what they should be doing based on the various research hypotheses. As we said, right at the top, it is humbling.

Tip   Try and keep the number of testers to around five or six. Any more than that and the odds are pretty good you will learn the same thing repeatedly. We also suggest team members. Friends and family are not to be included. They will most likely tell you what they think you want to hear.

An obvious question is: Are these things expensive? Not really. When first exposed to user testing and usability testing, it is common for people to assume they will be watching the test through a two-way mirror. Not anymore. In today's environment, usability tests are cheap and fast and will yield issues and insights that can be quickly addressed.

Some Testing Methods

There are a variety of tests you can run. What tests to undertake and when is decided during the planning phase. A testing regimen is usually tied to the scope and budget. Enterprise or more extensive projects may involve a comprehensive testing protocol. In contrast, smaller projects may require nothing more than a trip to the local coffee shop where you ask selected patrons to try something out. Making a trip to the local coffee shop is, by the way, known as guerrilla testing. What follows are some of the more common testing methods.

User Tests

User tests are commonly undertaken before the project moves into the design phase:

- *Usability testing*: This method involves observing users performing predefined tasks with your app and measuring their performance, satisfaction, and difficulties. These tests can be done in a formal setting or your conference room.

    An example of this technique would be performing a usability test using a paper prototype. At this stage of the process, a paper prototype allows the team to test their basic concepts and ideas. In addition, paper prototypes, being low cost, can be quickly iterated based on feedback, and significant design issues or flaws can be easily identified and fixed.

- *Interviews*: Usually conducted by a third party, users are asked open-ended questions about their experience, opinions, and suggestions regarding a product or service.

- *Surveys*: Surveys ask users closed-ended questions about their demographics, behavior, attitudes, and preferences regarding a product or service. Surveys are commonly used during the project's research phase but can be used as a "check-in" at various project stages.

- *Focus groups*: This method facilitates a discussion among users about their perceptions, expectations, and reactions to a product or service. Focus groups can provide deep insights into user needs, motivations, and emotions but can also be influenced by group dynamics and social desirability.

- *Card sorting*: This method (Figure 9-2) involves asking users or team members to sort a set of cards with labels or images into categories that make sense to them. Card sorting can help understand how users organize and structure information and can inform the design of navigation, content, and layout of a product or service.

  For example, each group member is handed a stack of cards with labels. The cards contain the various areas involved in setting up an account for the parking app. The labels on the cards could be Name and Address, Car Make, Car License Number, Credit Card, Username, and Password. They are then asked to arrange the cards in the order they would prefer to set up an account.

- *A/B testing*: This method involves comparing two versions of a product or service (A and B) with different features or designs and measuring how users respond to each version. A/B testing can help determine which version performs better regarding user engagement and other metrics.

  Though this testing method can be complicated, a simple example would be showing users two wireframe versions of the home screen and asking them to identify the version that works for them. For example, the A version could contain three buttons—Login In, New Account, and Learn More. The B version would only have the Login button with the New Account presented as a text link, and the Learn More button is also a link at the bottom of the screen. Next, the participants are randomly divided into two groups—A and B—and each group is presented with their respective screen and asked to provide feedback on the design, layout, etc. Once the results are in, the team knows which design is more practical, providing the path to improving the design.

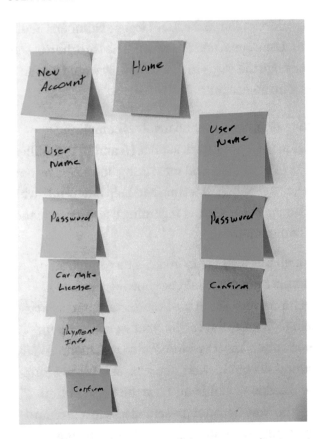

Figure 9-2. Card sorting gives users the opportunity to set preferred screen order

Usability Tests

Usability testing evaluates how easy and intuitive your product is to use by observing real users interacting with it. For example, it is common to hand the prototype to potential users, who are asked to perform certain tasks or "kick the tires." By doing this, you can identify problems and opportunities for improvement in the product's design, functionality, and user satisfaction. There are many methods of usability testing, but some of the more common ones are

- *Task analysis*: This method involves asking the user to perform a specific task or series of tasks and evaluating how well each is executed. The results can help identify a product's efficiency, effectiveness, and errors.

- *Eye tracking*: This method involves tracking and recording the users' eye movements as they use a product or service. In this way, you can observe the users' attention, focus, and interest.

- *Heat mapping*: Though sometimes equated with eye tracking, a heat map differs in how it works. Heat maps are created from mouse clicks or taps, movement, and scrolling. Their purpose is to give the team a deeper insight into which areas of the screen gain more user attention, clicks, taps, or interactions.

- *A/B testing*: This method involves comparing two versions of a product or service (A and B) to see which performs better on a specific metric or outcome. An A/B test can help determine a product or service's optimal design, feature, or content. A/B testing can be done online or offline, with large or small samples of users.

- *Remote testing*: This last method uses software or applications to watch users interact with the product. Prototyping software also contains features that will record a video of someone using the app, showing where their finger or mouse moves while performing specific tasks. The advantage to this is you can extend the geographic reach of the test in a very cost-effective manner.

Tip   Each of the tests presented also has accessibility implications. Be sure to test for accessibility at the same time.

Preparing to Test

There is no doubt that, when confronted with testing for the first time, it may strike you as being a rather complicated process. There are obvious questions you may have such as "How do we choose people to do the testing?", "Who will conduct the test?", "Where will the test be done?" These are valid questions.

The process is not complicated—and user testing or usability testing can be broken down into three steps:

- The first is pretest tasks, where you determine who will participate, where they will participate, and when. The questions to be asked and the tasks to be performed will also be determined.

- Next is the test itself.

- Following the test session, the results must be analyzed and priorities and opportunities identified.

Knowing what you are trying to discover makes sense if you plan to run a test. What you are looking for are actionable answers to the questions you will pose, and those questions may require the participants to undertake different tasks. For example, you might have a general question, such as how well users will identify the parking lot number, or more specific questions, such as how long it takes a user to find the section where they register a credit card. Bottom line? Asking the right questions and knowing how you will use the answers ensures you are asking questions with answers that can be measured. Nothing is more disheartening than completing a test and realizing there is not much there to improve the product.

For example, a test may reveal users have trouble identifying the lot number to be entered in the app. One possible solution would be to have the client change the lot signage to make the lot numbers more prominent. Another might be to use location tracking to do it for the user. In that case, the development team will have to find a way to do this.

By knowing the right questions to ask or tasks to be performed, a test will yield three crucial metrics: how long it took to complete a task, how many errors were made, and how satisfied or frustrated the testers were. When these three metrics are placed against their potential cost to address them when the product is released, it will give the team a very good idea of the priorities based on the results.

Two Low-Cost Testing Methods

We have concentrated on testing in this chapter and hope you have realized testing is something to consider at every project phase, from wireframes and paper prototypes to full-bore, high-fidelity, interactive prototypes. The reason is much like the one we use to justify motion. You can't assume how people will use your project. You have to see it. As we said earlier, watching users stumble through your project can be a humbling experience. Still, watching people use the interface is the only way to learn where the issues are and how to fix them. In many respects, this is where you fall in love with the user, not the technology.

We won't deny that the scope of regular testing is a function of budget because user testing techniques range from relatively inexpensive to hiring a usability testing service that will retain the testers best suited to the research. This group will institute a formal testing routine using a variety of tests designed to give all of the project's features a comprehensive run-through and then provide the team with the results. Two low-cost ways of conducting regular tests are Black Hat sessions and guerrilla testing.

The Black Hat technique is based on Edward de Bono's *Six Thinking Hats* developed in 1986. This is a team technique for critiquing a project. The person designated as the black hat is obligated to be brutally honest in pointing out the weaknesses in the UX design and layout, such as what is confusing or needs improving.

A Black Hat session is interesting because it permits anybody to give negative feedback and concerns to the team without consequences. It also provides the team with data points that can be tracked, managed, and if necessary... redone or refined.

Note   Many prototyping applications, such as Adobe XD, allow you to record people using the prototype. Recording the test allows the team to view how long it takes to complete a task and to see where stumbling blocks pop up.

Guerrilla testing is also rather interesting.

Guerrilla testing is what the name applies. You take a prototype to a coffee shop and ask random people if they'd be available to take 10 or 15 minutes to try out specific features of the project. If they agree, hit the Record button and let them stumble through the project. You only need to recruit five users for maximum results because after five people have tried it out, they will tell you what the first five people told you anyway. The advantages of guerrilla testing are that you quickly identify major usability issues as you move through the UX design process. If people are stumbling, you have a problem. Your assumptions are either proven or disproven. And if they are disproven, don't take them personally. It makes the case for user testing, especially for those with problems, acknowledging its importance.

> **Tip**   If you are doing guerrilla testing, gift cards are an excellent method of encouraging people to participate.

As you may have guessed, a wide variety of tests can be conducted at various points in the research, design, and development cycles. The type of test and how often the testing is done is strictly a function of budget. Earlier in this chapter, we outlined several of them. You may be wondering how does one conduct a test. Great question. Here are two tests and how they might be conducted. One is a user test done during conceptualization, and the other is undertaken during the design phase.

Conducting a Test Using a Paper Prototype

As we said earlier, "Test early and test often." One test that can be conducted before one pixel is lit up is to test using a paper prototype (Figure 9-3), which could be based on the wireframes. Testing using a paper prototype is a low-cost and effective way to evaluate the usability and feasibility of a design idea. A paper prototype is a mockup of the user interface made of paper or other materials that can be easily manipulated. The paper prototype can be used to simulate the interaction and functionality of the product. It is an excellent way of validating the team's initial hypothesis.

> **Tip**   An online collection of templates that you might find useful for creating paper prototypes is https://sneakpeekit.com.

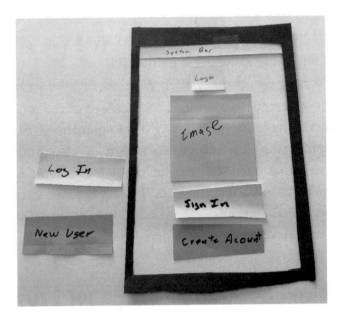

Figure 9-3. *Paper prototypes can be tested early in the conceptual phase*

To conduct a user test using a paper prototype... all you need is the prototype, someone to run the test, someone to perform the task and provide feedback, and a team member to take notes and observe the user's actions and comments. You also might want to record the session or have team members observe the test.

Performing the test requires a few things. First, the test environment should be free of distractions, and, if using a camera, ensure the participant's face and the prototype are in the frame. The tester should explain the purpose and goals of the test and what is expected. What is important is the user should know they are not there to test the design—it's too early for that—and there are no right or wrong answers.

With that out of the way, the test can begin. The user is presented with a realistic scenario and asked to perform the task using the prototype. For example, the user could be asked to select their vehicle using the wireframe of the screen requiring the user to do just that. If the participant has problems with that task or takes excessive time to find the vehicle, the tester should ask probing questions such as "Where were you first looking to find your vehicle?"

With the test completed, the participant should be thanked for their time and asked to share their impressions of the screen—what they liked, what they didn't like, what they found easy and what they found challenging, what they would like to change, or what needs to be improved. All of this feedback is invaluable information.

With the results compiled, any notes, recordings, and input from the user will provide the team with insights into the strengths and weaknesses of the concept. These data points can then be analyzed to refine the design and create a better prototype if another test is required.

Conducting an A/B Test

Running an A/B test compares two design versions to determine which performs better with users. For example, we mentioned earlier that users might have issues with the Confirm Payment button, and the decision is to change its color to ensure the button is more noticeable and will be tapped (Figure 9-4).

Figure 9-4. A/B tests determine user preference between two changes

These tests are not difficult to undertake but should be carefully planned. Here are some steps to take when conducting an A/B test:

- *Define the objective*: The first step is determining your goal with the A/B test, in this case to increase the number of payment confirmations.

- *Identify the variables*: Identify the variables you want to test in your design, such as the color of a button and its placement.

- *Create two versions*: Develop two versions of your design, version A and version B, with only one variable different between them.

- *Choose your sample*: Select a representative group of users who are representative of the audience and are large enough to ensure statistical significance.

- *Randomize*: Randomly divide the group to ensure design change reactions are measured, not preferences or biases.

- *Collect data*: Collect the same data from both groups. For example, the data could include user behavior, tap rate, etc.

- *Analyze the results*: Use statistical analysis to compare the data collected from both versions. This will help you determine which version performed better.

- *Draw conclusions*: Based on the results, determine which version is more effective and make changes accordingly.

- *Repeat*: If necessary, repeat the process with different variables, such as moving the button to a different position on the screen, until you achieve the desired outcome.

Remember, A/B testing should be a continuous process that helps you optimize your design for a better user experience.

As a developer, user tests can have profound or minor implications. For example, the A/B test determines the color of the Confirm Payment button should be changed and the button should be moved to a more prominent position. This change could ripple through the design system and require the front-end developer to reposition the button. However, in this case, the implications are relatively minor.

Let's now assume the testers questioned why this button exists in the first place. Their observation is that if they have chosen their duration and approved the payment from their account, this seems unnecessary. The UX design team has carefully considered this observation and concluded that it is not a necessary step and should be removed. Their recommendation is it be replaced with a modal notifying the user the session has started when they pay for parking. Obviously, this has profound implications ranging from the redesign of a screen to potential back-end payment changes.

This explains why the development team needs to be involved in the testing process. Not only do they see where the pain points are located; they understand why the change requests are being made. When the team gathers to discuss how to implement the changes, the development team, with the test results in hand, can actively participate in this discussion.

Tip   It isn't only elements and screens that can be subjected to A/B testing. Consider subjecting your user flows and task flows in the prototype to an A/B test.

It Is All About Context

Let's wrap up this chapter by discussing the importance of context in testing.

Most prototyping applications have a feature or plugin that lets you share the project to collect input and feedback. The recipient is provided with a link to open and then record how they perform specific tasks. These features are ideal for user testing because mouse or finger motion can be captured with clicks or taps as specific required tasks are completed. This feature makes conducting regular tests easier as the project moves through the production cycle. Though they are excellent tools, in many respects, the app being tested has no context other than showing up in an image of an iPhone or Google Phone.

As the production process moves closer to the finish, it is imperative that usability tests and accessibility tests be conducted on actual devices. iPhones are not Android devices; no two iPhones or Android devices are the same. Toss in the variety of tablets out there, and it becomes apparent device testing is critical.

Let's, for a moment, assume you target the iPhone 14 (Figure 9-5). You could realistically expect the UI will work on that version. Not so fast. That model has four versions, four different screen sizes, and two different pixel densities. Each of those differences could affect the usability of your project.

Display

Super Retina XDR display
6.1-inch (diagonal) all-screen OLED display
2532-by-1170-pixel resolution at 460 ppi

The iPhone 14 display has rounded corners that follow a beautiful curved design, and these corners are within a standard rectangle. When measured as a standard rectangular shape, the screen is 6.06 inches diagonally (actual viewable area is less).

Super Retina XDR display
6.7-inch (diagonal) all-screen OLED display
2778-by-1284-pixel resolution at 458 ppi

The iPhone 14 Plus display has rounded corners that follow a beautiful curved design, and these corners are within a standard rectangle. When measured as a standard rectangular shape, the screen is 6.68 inches diagonally (actual viewable area is less).

Figure 9-5. The iPhone 14 display and resolution specifications are different between versions (source: Apple.com)

Android is a completely different universe. The Google Pixel 7 (Figure 9-6) has two different screen sizes and pixel densities. The Samsung Galaxy Note 20 has two different screen sizes and pixel densities. And so it goes. Which to pick? Of course, not everyone has the latest and greatest, so the question becomes: How far back do you go to provide a consistently positive user experience? You also need to be aware that with the reintroduction of flip phones and now foldable phone devices, dimensions and interactions will need to be tested—collected data from a released app should include these specifics to help refine the app to meet the audience needs. We'll get into collecting user data in the next chapter.

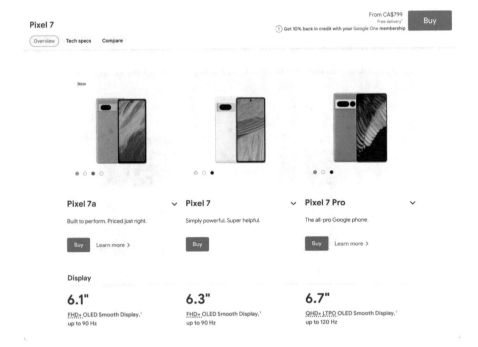

Figure 9-6. *The Pixel devices on Google's Pixel site all have different specifications*

When it comes to tablets, the same issues present themselves. On top of that, you need to test how the project functions in both portrait and landscape modes. Again, you have to determine which iOS and Android versions of the tablets are to be used for testing, and, again, how far back do you go to provide a consistently positive user experience?

These questions need to be answered right at the start of the process, not when you are ready to upload the app to the Apple App Store, Google Play, or a web server. When making those decisions, you also need to consider that a website will not always be viewed using a desktop browser. Websites are now viewed on tablets and smartphones, and it will be the development team that will handle this though the design team will create the prototype to guide the development team. If not, something that has happened to all of us will become evident. You encounter a button that is so small it is impossible to tap or text that is impossible to read. It is a pretty good assumption that these projects were not subject to "in-context" testing.

Conclusion

There has been a lot of ground covered in this chapter, and it started by clearly explaining the term "user testing" is commonly misunderstood. It is, in fact, only half of the testing protocol. User testing is done during the conceptual phase to validate the various hypotheses that spring from the research and the initial wireframes developed from the conceptual stage. Usability testing is conducted when the project moves into the design and development phase and should be a continuing process. As we pointed out, "user testing focuses on all users, while usability testing focuses on a specific segment of users."

We then moved into the various user and usability tests that can be undertaken. Though there are overlaps, the overlapping tests are used for different purposes.

From there, we presented how to prepare for a test. There are three steps:

- Pretest preparation where the participants and test location are selected, who will conduct the test is decided, and the questions to be asked or tasks to be performed are developed

- The test in which the moderator will ask probing questions and take detailed notes and, in many instances, the test will be recorded

- Analysis of the test results and prioritizing the issues raised

Obviously, testing has financial implications, and the breadth and depth of the testing regimen is tied to the budget. Realizing this, we presented two relatively low-cost approaches. The first was a Black Hat session, where a team member is permitted to question everything. In many respects, it reminds us of Hillman Curtis's "Justify" approach. The other was guerrilla testing. In this one, you go to the local coffee shop and ask the patrons to perform specific tasks. These two methods, obviously, are not meant to replace a comprehensive user and usability series of tests... but reveal essential data points regarding the project.

Rather than provide in-depth overviews of the various testing methods, we provided guidance around conducting a paper prototype user test and an A/B usability test. By presenting these, we gave you an idea of the difference between a user test and a usability test.

We concluded the chapter with a discussion of why "in-context" testing is also essential. Though the various prototyping applications lend themselves to user testing, they can only go so far. Your projects have to be subjected to usability testing on a variety of devices and platforms. This includes reminding you that websites are not always viewed in desktop browsers. Therefore, the various devices and the orientations need to be established at the outset of the conceptual phase and tested.

If there is one thing that is the "takeaway" from this chapter, it is this: Test early and often.

CHAPTER 10

Developer Handoff

*I believe, that developers are the end-users of designers'
mockups.*

—Helen Shabanova
"How to make programmers happy and
design-to-developer handoff less painful"
bootcamp.uxdesign.cc

A few years back, one of us was sitting in the audience during a local
meetup. This particular evening a developer was presenting a project their
team had been developing for a client. The author, along with the rest of
the audience, had to admit it was an incredible piece of work. That was
until the presenter said, "Of course we had some designers who did a great
job of handing the pretty pictures off to us for our code." Being a designer,
the author raised his hand to ask a question. "So tell me," he asked, "did
you get a call from the client praising you for those awesome algorithms
and optimized code that made the project run as smooth as silk?" The
question was met with silence on the part of the presenter. The author
continued, "Most likely not, but I am willing to bet the client heaped a
ton of praise on the designer." The developer replied with a rather crude
expletive, and that was that.

T. Green and J. Labrecque, *A Guide to UX Design and Development*, Design Thinking,
https://doi.org/10.1007/978-1-4842-9576-2_10

The point of this story is not to point out the arrogance of the developer. The point is, stroking his ego, the developer ignored the heart of the project's success. The project was a success because the development team were keenly aware of the designer's intent and had access to the prototypes at every step of the process. When it came time to hand the project off to the developer, they knew exactly what to do and with what.

Though this chapter deals with developer handoff, you need to know it doesn't happen when the prototype gets a signoff and is tossed into the laps of the developers. It starts when the relationships between the designers and developers are formed, which is usually before the start of the design process. By not forming these relationships right at the start, design is separated from implementation when they should be welded together. In short, prototype sharing should be a continuing dialog between design and development right from the start of the design process, which involves building and iterating together because visual and interaction design details reveal themselves over the duration of the design process.

As the design starts to come to life, involving the developers can yield significant benefits. Here's an example. The iOS version of the parking app is being designed, and the developer, seeing a prototype, adds a technical comment around waiting for the payment information to be accepted:

> "How long does it take for the API to grab the approval from the credit card vendor? If it takes too long, then a spinner might not be appropriate."

An initial response from the designer might be to ignore that comment. A wise designer understands what the developer is really saying is, "If the spinner goes on too long, users will think the application has crashed."

One company, Intercom, has formalized this process. A project starts with a discussion between the design and development teams as shown in Figure 10-1. The intermission is where a one-page project brief is produced. Then the designs are built. The development team makes suggestions as they iterate through the build. Once everyone is on board, they move the beta phase, and the design/build cycle restarts.

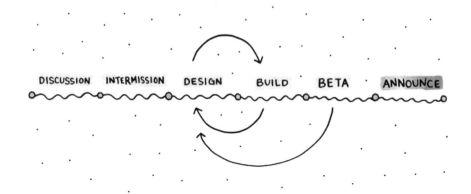

Figure 10-1. *The Intercom process is a collaborative effort between the design and development teams*

Though there is no standard workflow for handoff, here are some steps to consider:

- *Document the design*: Throughout this book we have been discussing and presenting the documentation that may need to be produced as you move through the UX Process. Preparing for the handoff to the development team is no different. It would be helpful to prepare a one- or two-page document that summarizes the design decisions behind the project. If the development team has been intimately involved in the process right from the start, this document will serve as reference more than anything else.

  This easy-to-read document could include details of the decisions made, the intended user flow, and any other information the development team may find useful. Most prototyping software contains a feature that allows for comments. The designers may use this feature to point out specific aspects of each screen such as colors, typography, and spacing guidelines. The neat thing about this is it really isn't necessary to print out annotated screenshots.

- *Organize the prototype*: This step essentially cleans up the prototype and asset files in a logical manner. For example, blank layers should be removed. Groups are clearly labeled and named. Layers and all asset files use a consistent naming convention. By doing this life is made easier for the developer because they will be able to navigate the project to find what is needed.

- *Label all elements*: If the designer hasn't done this, now would be a good time to complete this task. The elements should have descriptive labels that clearly state the purpose of that particular element. Parking.jpg may be a common name for an image, but it is useless when used in a UX project. A more appropriate name may be Parking_@2x.jpg. In this way the developer knows which version of the project uses this image.

- *Provide design specifications*: If you use a design system, this really isn't necessary because the development team will have access to it through GitHub or some other repository. By doing this the developer can implement the design accurately.

- *Export assets*: All assets used in the project such as images, icons, and logos should be ready to go in their proper format and size. This includes file formats such as SVG, JPG, PNG, and JSON for animations found in the prototype.

- *Let the software do the work*: Prototyping applications such as Adobe XD or Figma as well as applications such as Zeplin and Avocode do tend to streamline the handoff process. These software tools give the designer the opportunity to upload the design files, organize them, and provide the development team with the assets and specifications they need. The prototype will also allow the development team to inspect the code and extract the CSS or other code necessary.

All Platforms Are Not Created Equally

When projects are being developed for Apple's iOS, Google's Android, and the Web… a proper handoff to development is critical. For example, if a project includes a web version of the app, you simply can't assume it will only be viewed in portrait mode or that everyone will be using the same device. Toss in the full range of tablets, and things get messy. These are issues that should not be addressed at handoff but addressed right at the start of the UX Process. Having said that, it is not uncommon to open a web page on a smartphone and finding yourself pinching the screen to zoom in on a button or link that is barely visible, let alone is interactive.

Before we dig into iOS and Android, let's deal with the Web.

To start, it should not be your job to deal with responsiveness. It is incumbent upon the designers, with your input, to determine where the breakpoints are to be placed and the screens adjusted to accommodate those new screen dimensions. As we have repeatedly said, you have no control over the smartphone or tablet being used to view the content. This issue needs to be addressed right at the start of the design process. Of course, you can't accommodate every phone and tablet out there. Instead, pick a few target devices and design for them.

Though the days of browser "considerations" are somewhat behind us, being fixated on Chrome and Apple's Safari could be a huge mistake. Microsoft's Edge, Firefox, and Opera (Figure 10-2) are still out there and must be considered. Current desktop browser usage statistics, as of March 2023, show Chrome with a 65.4% market share, Microsoft Edge with 13.9%, and Safari with 10.3% with Firefox and Opera making up the rest.

Figure 10-2. *Global market share for the current, popular set of web browsers*

When it comes to tablets, Chrome and Safari account for 88.6% of the market with Chrome having twice the share of Safari. Smartphones have similar share with Chrome being almost 50% larger than Safari. These two browsers account for over 90% of the market. One browser, Samsung Internet, is on the radar with an almost 4% market share, which we suspect is due to the increasing popularity of these devices.

Though these statistics may make a compelling case for sticking with Chrome and Safari, keep in mind you have no control over which browser is being used to view your content.

When it comes to the CSS and HTML, as a developer, you can poke into the code generated by the prototype and choose to either use a snippet of the CSS... or to simply ignore it and do it yourself. One common feature of the prototyping applications is they do give you the spacing and margin measurements, which gives your workflow a significant boost in efficiency.

Apps are a totally different beast.

Apps have to be developed for the Android and iOS platforms. This means, as the developer, there are generally two different languages involved—Swift for iOS and Java/Kotlin for Android. When it comes to content, they have wildly differing scaling factors for imaging, and, when it comes to typography, the standard fonts are SF Pro for iOS and Roboto for Android. Though the default fonts are not platform-specific, SF Pro is designed for legibility at small sizes, whereas Roboto's letterforms are taller and provide a bit more space. Designers may or may not choose to use these fonts. In that case it might not be a bad idea to check if the fonts are properly licensed to avoid potential legal issues.

As the developer, it will be your responsibility to ensure the app is optimized for performance, meaning load times are minimized and the transitions between screens are smooth. This is commonly done by testing on a variety of target devices to ensure compatibility. One of the more common drags on load times is video. If you encounter this, possible solutions could be to reduce the bit rate for the video, reduce its physical dimensions to fit the screen, and, if there is an audio track, knock it back to mono from stereo. Another drag would be using PNG images for icons instead of SVG images. PNG images with transparency being used for icons are another drag on load times.

Bringing the Design System and UI Elements Together

Sticking a bunch of images, videos, audio files, and other assets such as icons into a folder and handing it over to you, the developer, sends you a rather disheartening message: "You figure it out." This of course is a nightmare scenario. Ensuring a smooth and effective handoff from design to development can be challenging. Do it right, and you can save time and money, reduce errors, and strengthen the collaboration between designers and developers.

A design handoff is the process of transferring the design specifications and assets to the developers who will implement them in code.

To ensure an effective handoff, here are some suggestions:

- *Organize and document the design assets*: First off, folders are wonderful tools, and all of the UI elements such as icons, images, audio and video, animations, and so on should be clearly named and placed in folders. Also make sure the designer has deleted any layers or files that are outdated or unused. Finally, ensure the files handed to the developer are pixel-perfect and aligned to a grid. Do this, and developers will find it a lot easier to find what they need. You also should agree to a common file and file folder naming convention.

- *Create a style guide*: It is all well and good to have the assets properly organized, but developers also need to know how they are used. A style guide such as one prepared in Storybook (Figure 10-3) not only outlines the design system but includes all the UI elements. It explains how each element is used and any design rules that should be followed. A concise style guide should be well-organized and easy to navigate and include clear descriptions and visual examples of each component and UI element.

- *Provide the design files*: It goes without saying all files should be in the proper format. These files can come from Sketch, Photoshop, or a prototyping application. As well... any asset files provided should have clearly named layers and provide the developer any external assets contained in the file.

- *Communicate*: Communication is the key to a successful handoff. Though such tools as Storybook are great ways of communicating the design language, the designer should clearly explain the design intent, logic behind the design decisions, and rationale to the development team. This is especially important if you are working from static designs from Sketch or another design tool. In this case, interactions and animations should be explained. We are not fans of static design because when it comes to interactions and animation, they are best shown, not described. This is the job of prototyping software. If there has been close communication between the development and design teams, it makes things a whole lot less complicated when it comes to resolving issues or conflicts during the handoff.

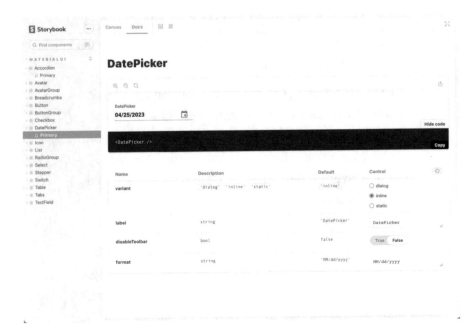

Figure 10-3. *A style guide organizer like Storybook documents use and provides code snippets*

The Front End and Back End Come Together

Once the design prototype is formally provided as a completed artifact to the development team—alongside additional documentation and other resources—it is time for the developers to shine. Of course, as expressed earlier, the development team will ideally have had many interactions and provided meaningful input into the entire UX Process from the very start—working closely with the designers during the user interface design and user experience design phases of the product lifecycle... But this phase is different. In this phase, it is all focused on true product development, and there are some definite considerations to be had when translating what you've been given into the finished product.

Let's have a look at both the considerations for front-end and back-end implementations and optimizations when translating the design prototype to a functional project.

Front-End Considerations

Since the front end is more immediate to the user, we'll look at that aspect first. Most of these concerns have to do with making the user feel comfortable within the experience and removing any roadblocks that may exist due to technology or design choices. As the developer, if problems are identified that should be brought to the attention of the design team for revisions... it is your responsibility to inform them as to what the issue is and what possible solutions exist and to be open for a discussion to come to an acceptable compromise.

When considering the front end, there are many things that are begging for attention... but they are generally covered across four different subjects:

- *Interface performance*: No one wants to experience a sluggish interface! Everything should feel snappy, immediate, and natural—no matter if the user taps, clicks, swipes, or interacts in any number of other ways. Depending upon the target platforms, you'll want to be sure that you are not making use of underlying systems that strain older hardware or are lacking in performance in aging versions of the operating system. As we'll see in Chapter 11, once you launch the product, it will be easier to know these specifics.

- *Responsiveness*: Whether your product targets the web browser, smaller mobile devices, or larger tablets... the application interface must take all of these resolution differences into consideration. Chances are that the design prototype provided is designed for a single screen size. All of those precise layout measurements can be dismissed for a more responsive implementation of the user interface elements on each screen. Often, there are mechanisms in the underlying platform that you can make use of to ensure everything the user sees is made responsive and can adapt to any screen size.

- *Accessibility*: Small text... tiny hit states... unfamiliar interface elements... these are all cause for concern when it comes to the overall usability of the experience. Not only must you ensure that the choices of things like text and UI hit states are acceptable to all demographics but consider also the user experiencing any of the elements present for the very first time. Would the user understand how to approach and use the various functions within the product? If there are blockers to the familiarity users will feel toward the experience... additional conversations may be in order, or retaining the services of an accessibility expert may help.

- *Documentation*: This is documentation for the user, which is normally meant for when the user first runs the application in order to become familiar with everything and to lead the user in identifying the primary functions of the experience. It often takes the form of an onboarding process or a built-in user guide. No matter how documentation is handled, it should be dismissible by the user and should never get in the way of the overall user experience.

Of course, there are additional things to consider when it comes to front-end implementation by the development team... but the items covered here should help inform whether you will need to look elsewhere or not (Figure 10-4). In either case, keep in mind the design team has no real way of monitoring these items—since prototyping software lacks the capabilities to do so. They rely upon you, as the developer, to identify whether any such problems exist so that they can be addressed in cooperation.

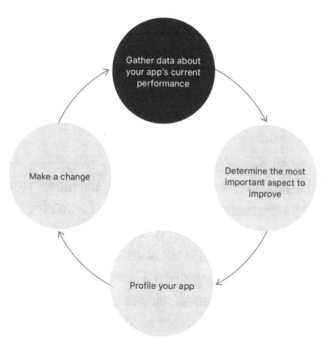

Figure 10-4. *When working on developing the front-end experience, it is entirely possible that changes will need to be made in implementation—either with the technology stack or even back with the overall design of the experience*

Back-End Considerations

While the front end is more immediate to the user experience—as least visually—the back end is often the source of even more concern due to the complexities with what is happening on the front end in addition to connections with the underlying hardware, operating system, and remote servers. In fact, there is likely much greater cause for product performance problems or even complete feature failure due to back-end issues.

Consider that the application requires a certain amount of CPU and memory to run efficiently... and our parking app, for example, will need to access back-end payment systems and authorization servers... If any link in this chain is performing poorly, the overall user experience will suffer. Major platforms such as Apple's ecosystem will supply developers with a number of tools to assist in monitoring and profiling both front-end and back-end processes.

Tip   While testing over and over by running the product and testing things individually—by yourself—can be an effective way to test both front-end and back-end functionality... you do not have to approach this task alone. Do not dismiss the tools that larger development platforms may provide (Figure 10-5) for testing very specific performance considerations and gathering data around other development insights. Apple is very good at providing a wide array of such tooling for their development platforms—but they are not alone in this!

Figure 10-5. *Many tools often exist for profiling not only back-end procedures and functions—but oftentimes there exist those for front-end processes as well*

When translating the functional features from the design prototype to a working application, the primary set of back-end considerations revolve around the following subjects:

- *Testing*: Write your tests from the very beginning. This will ensure that you do not have to go backward and write tests long after developing a lot of the code— playing catch-up—but that every function you write includes a corresponding test to ensure that as the systems become more complex, they are still working exactly as intended. Without proper tests in place... there are far too many unknowns.

- *Performance measuring*: You are often able to profile a number of processes that your product makes use of to identify any bottlenecks in performance. There are profiling tools for animation, CPU, GPU, remote

217

network traffic, and more. We will go into these in more detail a bit in the following—since it is such an important component of back-end performance.

- *Security*: Ensuring that your product is secure from outside threats is of utmost importance to your users—whether they know it or not. The worst publicity can be derived from some sort of security breach in your product... and that is something that is ultimately very difficult to recover from. Ensure you follow all guidelines and recommendations for the entire technology stack being used—and update your components to their latest versions to ensure any faults are up to date and patched by the provider.

- *Scaling for growth*: As you translate from a design prototype to a fully functional product... keep in mind that you have only a very faint idea before the initial release as to the growth projections of your user base. We'll see in Chapter 11 how to monitor your growth post-launch, but at this phase of the process... ensure that if you need to scale up quickly to support a massive influx of new users... this is the best time to prepare for such a possibility. Your technology choices should respect this possibility.

Very similar to front-end considerations, when making choices around back-end components to employ in your product development, a holistic view will benefit all aspects of the eventual product release—and the entire team and processes around it.

Tip   Always check the platform guidelines and developer documentation for every choice in your technology stack. There is important information on performance, design, and security concerns within such documentation that is ready for you to make use of before encountering any possible issues with your implementation.

In addition to what we've already covered, if problems are identified on the back end, you may need to dig deeper into the following areas:

- *Activity monitoring*: This is useful for features that require a request and response—such as when processing something like an availability or payment request over remote networks. Being able to trace your request from point to point and then verify a proper response is critical... especially when the exchange of money is involved (Figure 10-6)!

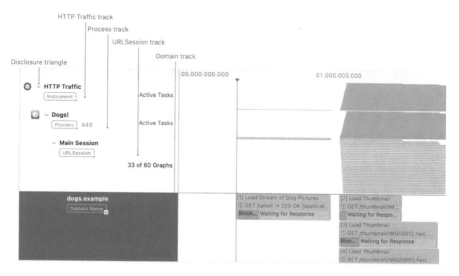

Figure 10-6. *An example of tracking HTTP traffic using Apple's network monitoring tools*

- *CPU/GPU profiling*: As mentioned when covering *performance measuring* earlier, profiling of specific hardware resources can help you determine how your application can be expected to run on different hardware. When you do launch across different platforms as the development cycle concludes... you can better determine what systems are most capable by using these tools—and can more properly catalog your product in the various app stores for the most appropriate users.

- *Memory leaks*: As a developer—you likely saw this one coming a mile away—often the most frustrating aspect of software development is identifying and tracking down memory leaks to resolve them. A memory leak can balloon into such monstrous problems that being able to keep an eye on memory and properly profile for any leaks—*from the start*—is a huge benefit to making use of any tools that are available on your chosen development platform.

As you likely already understand, translating a design prototype to a functional product is a massive undertaking. The considerations for performance, security, and accessibility across both the front end and back end can make or break the overall experience for your users.

Nothing Is Ever Finished

It would be a gross misconception to assume, once the project has been handed over to development, that it is time for the team to move on to the next project. It is the wise UX team that knows nothing is ever finished.

Things will change during development. Typos will be found. Blurry videos will need to be redone because they weren't encoded using square pixels. The client may change the brand color, a change that will ripple through the entire design system. User testing will reveal it takes an inordinate amount of time or steps to approve or complete a purchase. A new product is added to the client's product lineup. A major accessibility issue crops up. Think of something that could go wrong during development, and the odds are pretty good it just might. In many respects, as Helen Shabanova said right at the top of this chapter, developers are, indeed, the end users of a prototype.

The prototype is a reference tool used by developers to understand the design team's intent. It is the development team's job to bring focus to that broad "intent." There is a wide distance between "Here's what I think" and "Here's what it does." Along the way, there will be a plethora of issues to be resolved that require the same amount of collaboration and communication that has been evident throughout the entire process. In Chapter 1 we presented a classic example of this when a designer at Digg.com wanted to change the site's Digg button. The developer when presented with this request quickly quashed it, not because it was a change, but because it would require a major reformat of the code base and the server setup. Imagine the consequences if the developer had simply complied.

What developers and designers must understand is that apps and websites are not projects but what we call "living documents." One of us recently published an essay called "The Art of the Interactive Storyteller." The point was... stories never really have a point where one can add the traditional "The End." They can always be added to. Apps and websites tell stories, and they, too, due to regular changes and updates, never receive the proverbial "The End" until the app or website is withdrawn.

Adaptation is the key to development. The developer must have the ability to adapt to present and future changes. Present changes are easily accommodated, but future changes must also be considered. Here's an example:

One of us had acquired a Google Pixel because, knowing how the Android OS was constantly being updated, he wanted to stay current with the technology. Other Android devices didn't have this feature and were either lagging months behind the update cycle or their proprietary version of Android needed to be rewritten.

A few months ago, an app he used informed him it couldn't work with the current Android OS and to contact the vendor. Their response was basically "So what? We'll get around to it when we are ready." They really hadn't considered the implications of this response. They were immediately going to lose their Pixel customers and eventually their Android customers as the current Android version was rolled out during an update. The upshot was the author removed the app and the vendor lost a customer. As we made clear in the previous section, it is obvious the development team didn't consider scaling for growth.

That is a rather extreme example, but preparing to accommodate minor, major, and future changes after handoff is critical.

Conclusion

As you have learned in this chapter, handoff to development involves a lot more than prepping the assets and tossing them into development's arms with a cheery "Here you go."

Development handoff is a process that involves three continuous steps: design, build, and iterate. Repeat. To accomplish this... we suggested a six-step workflow:

- Document the design.

- Organize the prototype.

- Label all elements.

- Provide design specifications.

- Export the assets.

- Let the software do the work.

From there we explained how different operating systems and devices need to be accommodated, and, when the design system and other screen elements come together during handoff, we presented you with four items to consider prior to handoff. They are as follows:

- Organize and document the design assets.

- Create a style guide.

- Provide the design files.

- Communicate effectively and at all times.

With everything properly prepared, including the prototype that is now a reference tool, both the front-end and back-end development teams can get to work. Even so, as we point out: "In this phase, it is all focused on true product development, and there are some definite considerations to be had when translating what you've been given into the finished product."

We emphasized that, even though front-end development may be easier, there are four considerations that must be taken into account as development gets underway. They are

- Interface performance

- Responsiveness

- Accessibility

- Documentation

Back-end development is complicated. As we explained: "The back end is often the source of even more concern due to the complexities with what is happening on the front end in addition to connections with the underlying hardware, operating system, and remote servers. In fact, there is likely much greater cause for product performance problems or even complete feature failure due to back-end issues." To deal with this, we outlined four considerations when undertaking back-end development. They were

- Testing
- Performance measuring
- Security
- Scaling for growth

The chapter ended with a brief discussion of the overall process. What we made clear is that both the design and development teams must consider the handoff as a design/build/iterate/repeat process. Nothing is ever finished, and both design and development issues will crop up after handoff. As we said: "Preparing to accommodate minor, major, and future changes after handoff is critical."

They key to success is maintaining the continuous collaboration and communication developed right at the start of the UX Process.

CHAPTER 11

Release into the Wild and Beyond

Design isn't finished until somebody is using it.

—Brenda Laurel

We have come a long way in the course of this book: from research and discovery phases at the very beginning through considerations around design systems, UI design, UX design, development, user testing, and more... we've now arrived at the very end of the UX Process lifecycle and will discover whether all these decisions have led to a viable product for all stakeholders—or a complete dud to all.

With all this previously mentioned work completed... it is time for the moment of truth. Recall the minimal viable product (MVP) and how this has always been the focused target. A good enough product release is that which covers the features identified in your MVP and does so successfully. Having a concise and focused initial release is often not just good enough... but is, in fact, ideal for marketing and adoption purposes.

With the product release to actual users in the wild, you'll initially discover whether all of your struggles were worth the effort by the feedback provided by your users. As adoption (hopefully) increases, your team can monitor growth in installations and active usage alongside distribution

© Tom Green and Joseph Labrecque 2023
T. Green and J. Labrecque, *A Guide to UX Design and Development*, Design Thinking,
https://doi.org/10.1007/978-1-4842-9576-2_11

platform ratings and reviews. Of course, that is only part of the story... as built-in analytics can provide a less *emotional* response to the product release. Data from such analytics can be gathered and processed by your research team to inform not only the direction the product is heading... but it can give key insights into which technologies and platforms to support in future releases.

During all of this excitement, you must always keep an eye on the future and begin making decisions today as to the direction of the product, post-launch. Ideally, by the initial product launch, your team will have a road map in place that outlines both quality-of-life and feature-bearing updates.

We'll cover all of these concerns and more—within this final chapter.

A "Good Enough" Product Release

Now that we are at the end of our journey, let's revisit a concept from Chapter 3. Recall that the minimum viable product (MVP) should define all features necessary for users to successfully use your product without any additional features that might complicate matters or get in the way of the user flow. Your initial product release should aspire to match those features of the previously defined MVP in order to be "good enough" for a proper user experience.

When readying your product for release... look back to the MVP definition to determine whether it is truly ready to be presented to the world. Do you have the fully developed features that match those of the MVP? Do these features align with expectations expressed during the early phases of the UX Process? If there is any mismatch here, you may want to adjust your expectations or even revise the initial release in order to focus on only those features that constitute the MVP and might be considered "good enough" in the minds of most users (Figure 11-1).

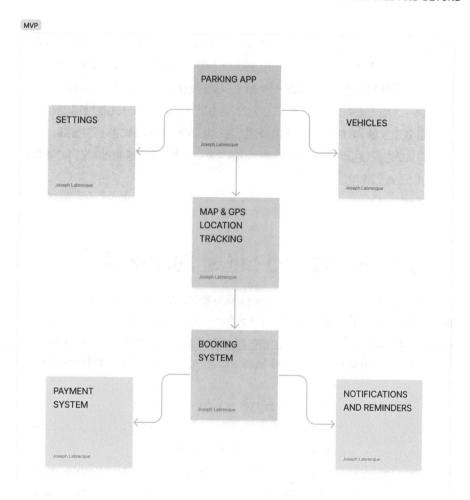

Figure 11-1. *Recall the definition of your MVP (minimum viable product)—this should be good enough for your initial release*

As we've seen in previous chapters, user testing can play a large role in determining whether the MVP is good enough for a positive user experience—or whether you may need to revisit certain aspects of the application during development. You only make a first impression upon your users once... so best to make it count!

Note   If you do find that there is a difference in the finished product, as developed, and the conceptual feature set established by the MVP… it is likely not a huge worry. User testing can alleviate any concerns that exist. If those concerns turn out to be actual issues, recall there is no shame in making a hard pivot to avoid disaster. Delaying a product launch to ensure everything is as solid as possible is not a bad thing!

Early Adopters and Initial Feedback

One of the first things you will want to do after releasing your product to the world is to gather initial feedback from your users. This loops us back to the beginning of this entire process when gathering UX research—but this time, we are on the other side of things as we can now collect data from actual users.

Recall that one of the primary ways of performing product research is to gather user reviews from app stores and such. We want to pay close attention to the reviews being given by early adopters to see how the product is being perceived. The two most important things to look for in user feedback are whether the user is able to effectively accomplish the function of the product… and how natural the experience felt to them. Positive feedback is wonderful, of course… but negative feedback is great, too, as it provides a chance for improvements to be made in future releases.

Note   "*Design isn't finished until somebody is using it*" is an interesting quote that emphasizes the importance of getting your product out there into the hands of users. After all, if no one is using your product… what is the point of this entire process? There is more to it than that though… as even in the final tasks associated with a product release, it doesn't hurt to reconsider certain design decisions—whether for a last-minute adjustment or when looking to a future release.

Keeping an eye on reviews and ratings that are submitted to stores like Apple's App Store and the Google Play Store (Figure 11-2) will provide early indicators as to how our product is performing.

Figure 11-2. *Distribution platforms such as Google Play can provide a good deal of insight into the positive and negative aspects of the user experience through ratings and reviews*

These distribution platforms include ratings and reviews built into their user-facing experiences, which can then be easily accessed by designers and developers through their respective consoles. Not only does this provide a way for users to rate and write about their experiences with your product, but each review offers additional insights into which particular version of the product is being rated, which device the user was running it on, which version of Android or iOS was installed at the time, and even more. There are also opportunities to reply to users' comments as well... to possibly gain more insight into any issues with product usage. You can also thank users with positive reviews to show your engagement with the community and seek opportunities for partnerships.

If your product is web-based and not distributed by any mobile app store, you will have to do a bit more digging to get the sort of public feedback that is so easy for mobile developers to gather. Consider elevating a survey link within the experience to gather similar feedback in a more direct way. This is especially useful if triggered once you are sure the user has spent adequate time within the experience.

Note   Early adopters are normally those users who will be the most enthusiastic about your product—in either a positive or negative way. The positive early adopters are often the key to evangelization and growing your overall user base... so it is incredibly important to listen to their needs and respond to them accordingly.

Additionally, these platform-specific resources provide dashboards that can surface anonymous data points such as number of installs (or even uninstalls!) over a certain period of time. You can gather a variety of useful statistics simply by users performing the everyday acts of installing or running your product. This data can then be gathered and parsed by stakeholders for further discovery (Figure 11-3).

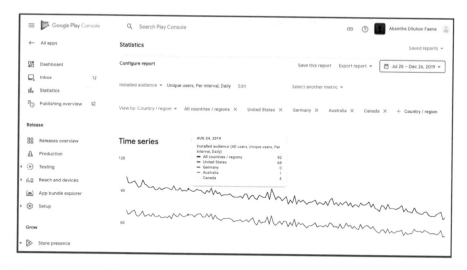

Figure 11-3. *The Google Play developer console can also provide a number of useful statistics across a large set of metrics*

Whether distributing your product through the Apple App Store or the Google Play Store, there exist a plethora of metrics that allow you to generate specific reports from both consoles. These insights can give you a clear idea of how quickly your product is being adopted over time—and can help your team plan their response to such growth. It can also reveal problems that may be occurring for users and give insight into how you might respond in correcting any issues through subsequent releases.

Some of these metrics (as surfaced within the Google Play developer console) include

- *Users*: This is the total number of users who have installed the product… and also the number who have uninstalled it. One of the most important metrics to keep an eye on as this is the primary indicator of growth over time.

- *Devices*: Similar to users but counts the number of total devices—as some users have multiple mobile devices such as a phone and tablet, perhaps even multiple phones if they use one for work and another for their personal time.

- *Engagement*: Measures statistics such as daily and monthly active users. If the user has your product installed but does not launch it… that will not appear within this metric. When you see this metric begin to drop… it means that users may be no longer interested in your app. Find out why!

- *Ratings*: Generally displayed as an average rating each day since the product launch date. While not detailed like a full review, this is a good indicator of user perception… and can give you an idea of how favorable users are toward your product.

- *Quality*: This is useful for determining the number of crashes and times the app has become unresponsive for your users. If you are seeing a lot of issues here… definitely time to identify and resolve them through an application update.

- *Pre-registration*: If you allow users to pre-register your app before launch, the number of pre-registrants is available for you here. Not very useful for anything other than the initial launch event.

- *Store list performance*: This is how many visitors to the public app store come in contact with your product listing. This metric has less to do with your product and much more to do with how effectively it is being marketed within a single platform.

All of these metrics (Figure 11-4) can be used following a product launch to monitor and respond to user impressions—whether positive or negative. Data around these impressions should be gathered by the research team and organized into something useful for all stakeholders to consider as new releases are planned.

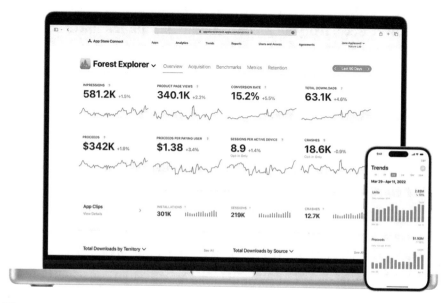

Figure 11-4. *A number of product release metrics are displayed as part of the Apple App Store developer console dashboard*

Tip   One invaluable data point is centered around device specifics. The ability to determine such aspects as the screen resolution and operating system versions of the majority of users running your app is incredibly useful. This can influence the road map of future versions in determining how the screen layout might shift based upon user screen specifics… and even whether it is safe to update frameworks and libraries being used, which may not support older versions of an operating system.

The users that install and use your product regularly from the very beginning can be your most loyal. These early adopters can sometimes make good partners for improving the product—as you can have one-on-one conversations with them about their experiences and what they think could improve the product. Certain users may hold a large presence on social media channels, and forming a relationship with them can influence the positive direction of your product considering the amount of influence certain people may have.

Making Use of Analytics Post-launch

Once your product finally lands in the hands of your users, you can gather a lot of data through direct feedback and user reviews—but do not forget to build rich, data-gathering analytics into the experience as well. Raw data such as this can be incredibly useful as it can reveal information about your users that they likely would not even consider sharing through direct feedback. This is especially true in terms of the more technical aspects of your users in what hardware and operating systems they are using to run your product.

Take something as ubiquitous as Google Analytics (Figure 11-5), for example. This service can be leveraged upon a general website, within specific installed applications, and even integrated as a personal feature in certain products and services that allow the users to track their analytics data. Using a service such as this, you can really drill down and define exactly the types of insights that can assist in determining the current performance of your product and also serve as a navigation mechanism for future decisions.

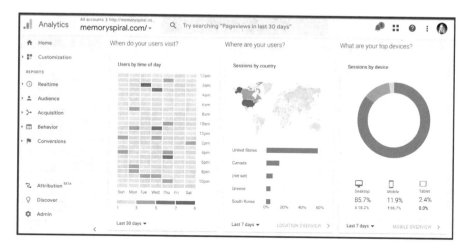

Figure 11-5. *Embedding analytics of some form into your product can provide many insights, post-launch*

Gathering such information can be critical to the post-launch success of your product—since there is no longer any speculation around user demographics or the hardware or software being used to run your application. In fact, all of the suppositions and assumptions made during the research phase of the project are either proven or disproven. Combining such analytics data alongside ratings, reviews, and user data gathered from various platform dashboards can really express a wealth of intelligence that would be difficult—if not impossible—to acquire otherwise. In many respects, being confronted with this hard data can be humbling.

As mentioned earlier… why not allow your users to tap into such analytics as well, when appropriate? If the application experience includes personal information—such as with a public-facing portfolio system (Figure 11-6)—then it is a benefit to your users to allow the same analytical introspection for their personal profiles that you might enjoy at an application level.

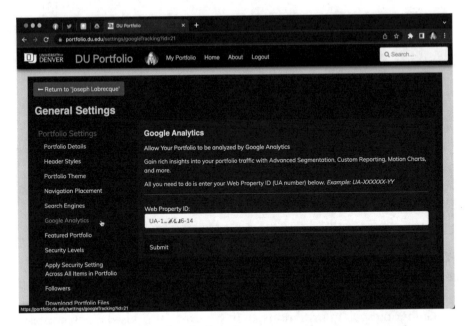

Figure 11-6. *An example of allowing users to leverage a service like Google Analytics as part of the user experience in an attempt to empower the user with additional, personal performance insights*

In fact, allowing users to tap into analytics in such a way can help establish a rapport with your users that can open up wider and more detailed conversations about your product and what the user would like to see in future developments. Of course, this sort of interaction is only feasible in services and products where it makes sense to implement such a thing, as in the portfolio example in Figure 11-6.

Apart from individual user concerns and curiosities, gathering such rich data can assist in the visualization of data insights to help eliminate any existing blind spots when assessing the current state of matters pertaining to your product. As well, this data becomes a resource behind the determination of future features along with your evolving product road map. There is nothing worse than remaining unaware that some problem exists simply because you do not have the proper insights to determine its existence… and the only way to correct any problem is to first recognize it for what it is.

Tip   Be transparent with your users when you do employ analytics gathering—whether in an app or through the Web. You do not want your users to distrust your intentions, and many people do not understand the benefits to tracking certain activities through mechanisms such as this. Request that the design team comes up with some information the user can access that explains briefly what information is gathered and for what purposes. This way, everything is transparent to the user, and the level of mistrust can be minimized.

Product Road Map and Planned Features

The last thing to consider at this point in the process can be summed up in two words: *What's next?* The best way to plan out new releases of your product is to start the process while considering your MVP all the way through to the initial release.

Your team and your client will inevitably begin considering new features and ways to expand the service offerings for your product as you build out the features defined in the MVP—but the initial release is not the time to load the product up with as much as possible... so these ideas are better used as features plotted along a road map as you all consider what happens post-launch. For the development team, when in the midst of building out the MVP features... take time to consider which additional ideas might make sense in future releases and how they may best be implemented.

Tip   Perhaps certain features are dependent upon others already being place… or are maybe reliant upon updated libraries and frameworks that are on the road map for later releases. Being aware of feature ideas from all stakeholders and planning for these possibilities while in the midst of foundational development can make implementation of these features much easier down the road—as you can prepare for them now.

No matter how your team and other stakeholders decide to organize these ideas for future releases, it is beneficial to everyone involved to begin establishing a product road map (Figure 11-7). As features or other updates are conceived and their particulars are solidified, determining which planned release makes the most sense for any particular update can be beneficial to everyone involved in the process—even the users if you choose to share upcoming and planned features with your user base.

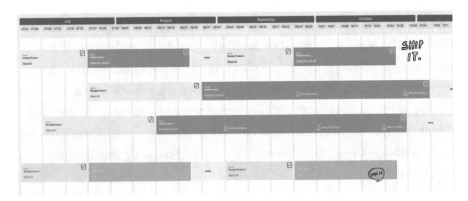

Figure 11-7. *Even prior to your initial release, a product road map and scheduled set of releases are a beneficial asset to establish and update as work progresses*

Tip As we've emphasized continuously throughout this book, forming relationships between teams and getting all stakeholders involved in process discussions can have great benefits to the overall success of your project. Planning for the future is no different—and with everyone being able to understand the goals and communicate their ideas… a solid product road map can be obtained with as little confusion and conflict as possible.

Conclusion

In this final chapter, we covered everything to consider when finally launching your project—from what constitutes a "good enough" release to gathering insights from platform consoles and even built-in analytics… to finally addressing why a product road map is important for both feature-bearing and more service-oriented releases of your product. You may think your job is done. It isn't. The post-release data actually continues the iterative process of design-build-develop as it reveals new opportunities and features that will enrich the user experience.

This brings us to the end of this book and the end of the developer's progress through the UX Process.

Throughout this book we have used the analogy of regarding the UX Process as a journey, and, like most journeys, it starts with a mission. In very simple terms, the UX Mission is to reach the end of the journey and, along the way, create an app or website that provides users with a positive experience. It is a deliberately vague statement, but it does point to the end result of the journey.

Like all journeys, there are rest stops, challenges, and guideposts along the way. The rest stops are research, design, and build. The challenges are complex and range from identifying who those users really are, what they really want, how they will use the product, and how the product will function. The guideposts are the documentation that needs to be created and explain how to meet the challenges.

Journeys are traditionally regarded as a straight line from "here to there." The UX journey, as you have learned, is not a straight line. It meanders through the rest stops and, more often than not, loops back on itself as constant testing reveals flaws that, in many cases, prevent you from moving forward to the next rest stop.

As the developer progresses through the process, others will join the journey. They are the all-important artisans who will work with the developer to achieve the mission. These artisans are the researchers, front-end and back-end developers, designers, motion designers, writers, and so on... all of whom are led throughout the journey by a UX Designer. It is the UX Designer who will determine the mission and take the first step along the path to accomplish it.

When you reach the end of the journey, it is only natural to stop and reflect upon the path taken—and your progress along that path. You will reflect on the pain, the joy, the exhilaration, and the satisfaction of having traveled the path. Most of all, you will have discovered just how much fun it was to work with your fellow travelers to create something new and unique.

We agree, and as we say at the end of each book we write

The amount of fun you can have in this business should be illegal. If you agree, we'll see you in jail.

Index

A

Adopters/initial feedback

B, C

D, E, F

Deep dive process
Design systems

© Tom Green and Joseph Labrecque 2023
T. Green and J. Labrecque, *A Guide to UX Design and Development*, Design Thinking,
https://doi.org/10.1007/978-1-4842-9576-2

W, X, Y, Z

Printed in the United States
by Baker & Taylor Publisher Services